SpringerBriefs in Computer Science

Series Editors

Stan Zdonik
Peng Ning
Shashi Shekhar
Jonathan Katz
Xindong Wu
Lakhmi C. Jain
David Padua
Xuemin Shen
Borko Furht
V. S. Subrahmanian
Martial Hebert
Katsushi Ikeuchi
Bruno Siciliano

For further volumes:
http://www.springer.com/series/10028

Ester Martínez-Martín
Ángel P. del Pobil

Robust Motion Detection
in Real-Life Scenarios

 Springer

Ester Martínez-Martín
Department of Computer Science and
    Engineering
Jaume I University
Av. de Vicent Sos Baynat, s/n 12071
Castellón de la Plana
Spain

Ángel P. del Pobil
Department of Computer Science and
    Engineering
Jaume I University
Av. de Vicent Sos Baynat, s/n 12071
Castellón de la Plana
Spain

ISSN 2191-5768   ISSN 2191-5776   (electronic)
ISBN 978-1-4471-4215-7   ISBN 978-1-4471-4216-4   (eBook)
DOI 10.1007/978-1-4471-4216-4
Springer London Heidelberg New York Dordrecht

Library of Congress Control Number: 2012940960

Printed on acid-free paper

Springer is part of Springer Science+Business Media (www.springer.com)

To my loving parents, Manolo y Fina, for walking with me in the life way, helping me to face up difficulties and magnifying my happiness. Everything I have with both of you is worth it

Ester

To Azucena, for her unconditional love and understanding

Angel

Preface

Our knowledge of the surrounding world is obtained by our senses of perception. Among them, vision is undoubtedly the most important for the information it can provide. In artificial systems, this discipline, known as Computer Vision, mainly tries to identify physical objects and scenes from captured images to be able to make useful decisions. For that, the processing and analysis of images, video sequences, views from multiple cameras or multi-dimensional data like a medical scanner, are carried out.

In this context, motion plays a main role since it provides a stimulus for detecting objects in movement within the observed scene. Moreover, motion allows obtaining other characteristics such as, for instance, object's shape, speed or trajectory, which are meaningful for detection and recognition. Nevertheless, the motion observable in a visual input could be due to different factors: movement of the imaged objects (targets and/or vacillating background elements), movement of the observer, motion of the light sources or a combination of (some of) them. Therefore, image analysis for motion detection will be conditional upon the considered factors. In particular, in this manuscript, we have focused on motion detection from images captured by perspective and fisheye still cameras. Note that, as cameras are still, egomotion will not be considered, although all the other factors can occur at any time.

With that assumption, we propose a complete sensor-independent visual system which provides a robust target motion detection. So, first, the way sensors obtain images of the world, in terms of resolution distribution and pixel neighbourhood, is studied. In that way, a proper spatial analysis of motion can be carried out. Then, a novel background maintenance approach for robust target motion detection is implemented. On this matter, two different situations will be considered: (1) a fixed camera observing a constant background where interest objects are moving; and, (2) a still camera observing interest objects in movement within a dynamic background. The reason for this distinction lies on developing, from the first analysis, a surveillance mechanism which removes the constraint of observing a scene free of foreground elements during several seconds when a reliable initial background model is obtained, since that situation cannot be guaranteed when a robotic system works in an unknown environment. Furthermore, on the way to achieve an ideal background maintenance system, other canonical problems are addressed such that the proposed approach successfully deals with (gradual and global) changes in illumination, the distinction between foreground and background elements in terms of motion and motionless, and non-uniform vacillating backgrounds, to name some.

The methods proposed in this book provide important advances with respect to state-of-the-art computer vision approaches to motion detection. Our algorithms allow a good environment adaptation of the system as it properly deals with most of the vision problems when dynamic, non-structured environments are considered. All these contributions are validated with an extensive set of experiments and applications using different testbeds of real environments with real and/or virtual targets.

Castellón de la Plana, Spain, June 2012   Ester Martínez-Martín
                                                                                    Angel P. del Pobil

Acknowledgments

There are a large number of people without whom this work could not have been carried out. We would like to express our deepest thanks and appreciations to those who gave us constant encouragement, tireless support, inspiration and motivation.

The research work described in this book has been conducted at the Robotic Intelligence Laboratory at Universitat Jaume-I (Castellón de la Plana, Spain). We would like to thank all its members as well as all the department colleagues, since all of them have collaborated in some way to make this work a reality, especially Dr. María de los Ángeles López Malo by means of her kind assistance and suggestions.

Furthermore, during the development of this work, we have collaborated with the Department of Interaction Science of Sungkyunkwan University (South Korea). That collaboration gave us the opportunity to meet a very different culture and great people. Among them, we would like to express our gratitude to Prof. Sukhan Lee, who offered us the opportunity of working at the Intelligent Systems Research Center. Thanks also to the administrative staff for all the assistance we received from them at every moment, and to all the members of the Department, especially to Dr. Yu-Bu Lee, who worked close to us, and Mr. Dongwook Shin for his kind help and friendliness.

Finally, this work would not have been possible without the financial support received from the World Class University (WCU) program through the National Research Foundation of Korea funded by the Ministry of Education, Science and Technology (Grant No. R31-2008-000-10062-0), from Ministerio de Ciencia e Innovación (DPI2011-27846), from Generalitat Valenciana (PROMETEO/2009/ 052) and from Fundació Caixa Castelló-Bancaixa (P1-1B2011-54).

Contents

Chapter 1
Introduction

Abstract One of the most challenging issues in computer vision is *image segmenta-tion*. The reason lies on the information it can provide about the elements in the scene from the automatic image division based on pixel similarities. Therefore, what makes a pixel interesting depends on the object's features to be considered. Thus, due to segmentation of countless applications, a wide range of solutions have been pro-posed and tested by the scientific community during the previous years. However, considering motion as a primary cue for target detection, background subtraction (BS) methods are commonly used. In this chapter, we overview the method in gen-eral terms as well as its different variants with the aim to analyze the problems remaining to be solved.

Keywords Machine vision · Computer vision · Image segmentation · Background subtraction · Motion detection · Robot vision · Dynamic environments · Visual surveillance

1.1 Background Subtraction Overview

Motion detection is the core of multiple automated visual applications by providing a stimulus to detect objects of interest in the field of view of the sensor. Such detection is usually carried out by using background subtraction (BS) methods, especially for applications relying on a fixed camera. Basically, the idea behind this kind of techniques is to first build a background model from a sequence of images in order to find the interest objects from the difference between that background estimation and the current frame.

Therefore, the accuracy of the segmentation process depends on how well the background is modeled. In addition, the problem gets more complex when real-life scenarios are considered. Actually, natural scenes are usually composed of several dynamic entities. For that, the estimated model should properly describe the scene

E. Martínez-Martín and A. P. del Pobil, *Robust Motion Detection in Real-Life Scenarios*, SpringerBriefs in Computer Science, DOI: 10.1007/978-1-4471-4216-4_1,
© Ester Martínez-Martín 2012

background which can change due to the presence of moving objects (e.g. swaying vegetation, fluctuating water, flickering monitors, ascending escalators, etc.), because of camera oscillations, due to changes in illumination (gradual or sudden) or in the background geometry such as parked cars, and so on.

With the aim to deal with those challenges, numerous methods have been proposed to date. These methods can be classified following the model used for the background representation as follows:

- *Basic background modeling.* the average [1], the median [2] or the histogram analysis over time [3].
- *Statistical background modeling.* the single Gaussian [4], the Mixture of Gaussians [5] or the Kernel Density Estimation (KDE) [6].
- *Background estimation.* Wiener filter [7], Kalman filter [8] or Tchebychev filter [9].

However, despite the wide research done in this area, there are still some problems that have not been addressed by most BS algorithms. Among them, we can find the quick illumination changes, the proper update of the background model when a background object is relocated, the initialization of the background estimation when moving objects are present in the scenes, or the shadows. Here, we propose a novel BS technique which is robust and generic enough to handle the complexities of most natural dynamic scenes. On this matter, two different situations have been considered: (1) a fixed camera observes a constant background where interest objects are moving; and, (2) a still camera observes interest objects moving in a dynamic background. The reason for this distinction lies on developing, from the first analysis, a surveillance mechanism that removes the constraint of observing a scene free of foreground elements during several seconds when a reliable initial background model is obtained, since that situation cannot be guaranteed when a system works in real-life scenarios. Furthermore, on the way to achieve an ideal motion detection process, other canonical problems are addressed such that the proposed approach successfully deals with (gradual and global) changes in illumination, distinction between foreground and background elements in terms of motion and motionless, and non-uniform vacillating backgrounds, to name some.

As the validation of the system with an extensive set of experiments and applications using different testbeds of real environments with real and/or virtual targets will show, the proposed motion detection algorithm allows a good environment adaptation of the system by properly dealing with most of the vision problems when dynamic, non-structured environments are considered.

References

1. Lee, B., Heddley, M.: Background estimation for video surveillance. In: Image and Vision Computing New Zealand (IVCNZ), pp. 315–320. Auckland, New Zealand (2002)
2. McFarlane, N., Shofield, C.: Segmentation and tracking of piglets in images. In: British Machine Vision and Applications (BMVA), pp. 187–193 (1995)

3. Zheng, J., Wang, Y., Nihan, N., Hallenbeck, E.: Extracting roadway background image: A model based approach. Journal of Transportation Research Report (1944), 82–88 (2006)

4. Wren, C., Azarbeyejani, A., Darrell, T., Pentland, A.: Pfinder: Real-time tracking of the human body. IEEE Transactions on Pattern Analysis and Machine Intelligence (PAMI) **19**(7), 780–785 (1997)

5. Stauffer, C., Grimson, W.: Adaptive background mixture models for real-time tracking. In: IEEE Conference on Computer Vision and Pattern Recognition (CVPR), pp. 246–252 (1999)

6. Elgammal, A., Harwood, D., Davis, L.: Background and foreground modeling using non-parametric kernel density estimation for visual surveillance. In: IEEE Proceedings, pp. 1151–1163 (2002)

7. Toyama, K., Krum, J., Brumitt, B., Meyers, B.: Wallflower: Principles and practice of background maintenance. In: Seventh IEEE International Conference on Computer Vision (ICCV), vol. 1, pp. 255–261. Kerkyra, Greece (1999)

8. Messelodi, S., Modena, C., Segata, N., Zanin, M.: A kalman filter based background updating algorithm robust to sharp illumination changes. In: 13th International Conference on Image Analysis and Processing (ICIAP). Cagliari, Italy (2005)

9. Chang, R., Ghandi, T., Trivedi, M.: Vision modules for a multi-sensory bridge monitoring approach. In: IEEE conference on Intelligent Transportation Systems (CITS). Washington DC, USA, October (2004)

Chapter 2
Motion Detection in Static Backgrounds

Abstract Motion detection plays a fundamental role in any object tracking or video
surveillance algorithm, to the extent that nearly all such algorithms start with motion
detection. Actually, the reliability with which potential foreground objects in movement can be identified, directly impacts on the efficiency and performance level
achievable by subsequent processing stages of tracking and/or object recognition.
However, detecting regions of change in images of the same scene is not a straightforward task since it does not only depend on the features of the foreground elements,
but also on the characteristics of the background such as, for instance, the presence
of vacillating elements. So, in this chapter, we have focused on the motion detection problem in the basic case, i.e., when all background elements are motionless.
The goal is to solve different issues referred to the use of different imaging sensors,
the adaptation to different environments, different motion speed, the shape changes of
the targets, or some uncontrolled dynamic factors such as, for instance,
gradual/sudden illumination changes. So, first, a brief overview of previous related
approaches is presented by analyzing factors which can make the system fail. Then,
we propose a motion segmentation algorithm that successfully deals with all the
arisen problems. Finally, performance evaluation, analysis, and discussion are carried out.

Keywords Motion detection · Background subtraction · Visual surveillance · Image
segmentation · Computer vision

2.1 State of the Art

Motion detection plays a fundamental role in any object tracking or video surveillance
algorithm, to the extent that nearly all such algorithms start with motion detection.
Actually, the reliability with which potential foreground objects in movement can
be identified, directly impacts on the efficiency and performance level achievable

E. Martínez-Martín and A. P. del Pobil, *Robust Motion Detection in Real-Life Scenarios*,
SpringerBriefs in Computer Science, DOI: 10.1007/978-1-4471-4216-4_2,
© Ester Martínez-Martín 2012

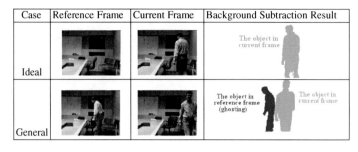

Fig. 2.1 Background subtraction results by depending on foreground presence/absence in the reference frame when a background(-frame) subtraction technique is used

by subsequent processing stages of tracking and/or recognition. However, detecting regions of change in images of the same scene is not a straightforward task since it does not only depend on the features of the foreground elements, but also on the characteristics of the background such as, for instance, the presence of vacillating elements. In this chapter we will study the motion detection on static scenes, that is, the only elements in movement will be the targets. In that way, it is possible to analyze and solve issues relative to the use of different imaging sensors, the adaptation to different environments, and to some dynamic, uncontrolled factors such as (gradual or global) changes in illumination.

From this starting point, any detected changed pixel will be considered as part of a foreground object. For that reason, techniques based on temporal information by using a thresholded frame difference could be fitted. By depending on the temporal relationship between frames implied in the difference, two different approaches can be defined. On the one hand, *background(-frame) subtraction* uses a reference frame to represent the scene background. That frame is usually set to the first captured image. Thus, a pixel is classified as foreground if its current value is considerably different from its value in the reference frame. Although it could seem the perfect solution, it is worth noting that two different situations can take place in real environments (see Fig. 2.1):

1. *Ideal situation.* There are no foreground objects in the reference frame. In this case, the resulting image would be the same as the desired segmentation result
2. *General situation.* Foreground objects may appear in the reference frame. Their presence makes background subtraction fail by providing false positives due to their position in the reference frame.

On the other hand, *techniques based on temporally adjacent frames* could be considered. Basically, this time-differencing approach suggests that a pixel is moving if its intensity has significantly changed between the current frame and the previous one. That is, a pixel x belongs to a moving object if

$$|I_t(x) - I_{t-1}(x)| < \tau \qquad (2.1)$$

Fig. 2.2 Drawbacks of adjacent frame difference approach

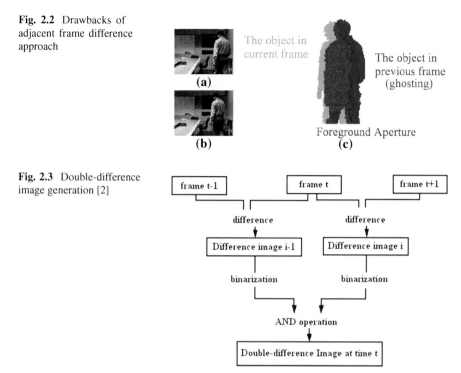

The object in current frame

The object in previous frame (ghosting)

(a)

(b)

Foreground Aperture

(c)

Fig. 2.3 Double-difference image generation [2]

where $I_t(x)$ represents the intensity value at pixel position x at time t and τ corresponds to a threshold describing a significant intensity change.

Nevertheless, in spite of the fact that this method provides an easy, fast moving object detection, it only works on particular conditions of object's speed and frame rate because they generate its two well-known difference drawbacks [1]: *ghosting* and *foreground aperture*. So, as depicted in Fig. 2.2, the presence of an object in the previous frame generates false alarms (*ghosting*), while the similarity between pixels when object's speed is too low or it becomes motionless, generates holes in the segmentation result (*foreground aperture*).

Thus, as a solution, Kameda and Minoh [2] proposed a variation of this method: a *double-difference* image. This approach operates a thresholded difference between frames at time t and $t - 1$ and between frames at time t and $t + 1$, by combining them with a logical **AND** (see Fig. 2.3). However, the object's position is not estimated in real time, an accurate motion detection is not allowed if the moving objects have no enough texture, and the situation in which targets become motionless is not considered.

In the *VSAMproject*, Collins et al. [1] described a different hybrid algorithm for motion detection. Basically, a three-frame differencing operation, based on image difference between frames at time t and $t - 1$ and the difference between t and $t - 2$, is performed to determine regions of legitimate motion and to erase *ghosting* problem. Then, an adaptive background(-frame) subtraction, proposed by Kanade et al. [3], was used to solve the *foreground aperture* problem. Nevertheless, although the proposed algorithm solves issues of image difference and gives good results in motion detection, the background update procedure fails when objects begin or end their motion and/or there are luminance variations in the scene. Moreover, it suffers a few drawbacks on variable depth shots since it was widely used in outdoor environments with a low depth of field images.

With the aim of solving these problems, many techniques for a proper background update have been developed. The simplest ones update the background by a convex composition of background pixels a time $t-1$ and those at time t such that the update weight for background pixels is eventually variable with pixel classification (light weight for background pixels and heavy weight for foreground pixels).

On the contrary, Migliore et al. [4] claimed that it is possible to obtain a robust pixel foreground classification without the need of previous background learning. For that, they exploited a joint background subtraction and frame-by-frame difference to properly classify pixels (see Algorithm 1). Then, the background model is selectively updated according to such classification as pointed out by Wren et al. [5], by using the following formula:

$$B_t = (1 - \alpha)B_{t-1} + \alpha F_t \tag{2.2}$$

where the α value is different depending on pixel classification. So, it is set to 0 if the pixel is classified as foreground by avoiding the background corruption; a low, non-zero value is used to slowly update the model; and, finally, in the case when any background element starts moving, a high α will allow to quickly restore the background model.

Algorithm 1 Joint Difference Algorithm [4]

---

if $((|F_t(x) - B_{t-1}(x)| > \tau_B)$ AND $(|F_t(x) - F_{t-1}(x)| > \tau_A))$ **then**
  Foreground Pixel;
else if $((|F_t(x) - B_{t-1}(x)| > \tau_B)$ AND $(|F_t(x) - F_{t-1}(x)| < \tau_A))$ **then**
  Collect pixels in blobs;
  if ($\sharp$ Foreground Pixels $\geq (\gamma * (\sharp$ Total Pixels$)))$ **then**
    Foreground Pixel; //foreground aperture problem solution
  else
    Background Pixel; //a background object suddenly starts moving at time t
  end if
else if $((|F_t(x) - B_{t-1}(x)| < \tau_B)$ AND $(|F_t(x) - F_{t-1}(x)| > \tau_A))$ **then**
  Background Pixel; //ghosting problem solution
else
  // $|F_t(x) - B_{t-1}(x)| < \tau_B$ AND $|F_t(x) - F_{t-1}(x)| < \tau_A$;
  Background Pixel;
end if

However, despite its good performance, it has two important handicaps. On the one hand, this method fails when a target stops or their speed is low. On the other hand, given that difference thresholds are established for the whole image, various factors, such as nonstationary and correlated noise, ambient illumination, inadequate contrast, and/or an object's size not commensurate with the scene, can make the approach fail.

2.2 Combination of Difference Approach

Our contribution at this stage is to provide a real-time algorithm for robust motion detection. For that, a combination of difference (CoD) techniques is proposed since it was proven that they provide a good performance. As presented by Migliore et al. [4], it is possible to overcome *adjacent difference* problems by using a *background(-frame) subtraction*.

The first issue to be solved is how to properly choose the threshold value because it is a key parameter in the segmentation process since it can affect quite critically the performance of successive steps. Although users can manually set a threshold value, it is not a valid solution when autonomous systems are designed. In this context, a common solution is to use a thresholding algorithm that automatically computes that value.

Sezgin and Sankur [6] categorized automatic thresholding methods according to the information they are exploiting, in:

- *Histogram shape-based methods*, where, for example, the peaks, valleys, and curvatures of the smoothed histogram are analyzed
- *Clustering-based methods* divide the gray-level samples into two parts (background and foreground), or alternately are modeled as a mixture of Gaussians
- *Entropy-based methods* result in algorithms that use the entropy of the foreground and background regions, the cross-entropy between the original and binarized image, etc.
- *Object attribute-based methods* search a similarity measurement between the gray-level and the binarized images such as fuzzy shape similarity, edge coincidence, etc.
- *The spatial methods* use higher order probability distributions and/or correlation between pixels
- *Local methods* adapt the threshold value on each pixel to the local image characteristics.

Despite the wide variety of possibilities, the existing methods only work well when the images to be thresholded satisfy their assumptions about the distribution of the gray-level values over the image. So, situations such as shape deformations of the interest object, the relationship of the foreground object's size with respect to the background, or overlapping of background and target gray-level distributions, make them fail. For all that, it was necessary to design a new way to automatically obtain the threshold value.

Our contribution at this point is an adaptive *dynamic* thresholding method such that it is capable of adapting to non-uniform-distributed resolution, inadequate illu-

Fig. 2.4 Perspective projection model

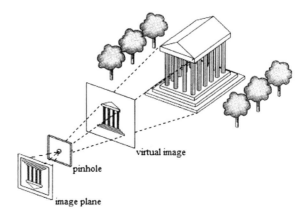

mination gradient in the scene, shadows, and gradual as well as sudden changes in illumination. The main idea is to divide each captured image in regions such that a threshold is obtained for each described area. A key issue is the way regions are defined since it is resolution-dependent and, therefore, camera-dependent. In this manuscript, two different kind of cameras are considered:

1. *Perspective cameras*, often referred as *pinhole cameras*, are optical imaging devices which follow the perspective projection model in order to obtain an image (see Fig. 2.4). Basically, the beams of light bouncing off an object are redirected by a lens to the image plane as if it was a rectilinear propagation of light through a small hole

2. *Fisheye cameras*, on the contrary, are imaging systems combining a fisheye lens with a conventional camera. They are usually used to present a small display of a large structure. For that, they use a lens with a wide field of view (*fisheye lens*) that allows them to take a hemispherical image. Their main advantages with respect to the catadioptric sensors (i.e., the combination of a conventional camera and mirrors) are, first, that they do not exhibit a dead area, and, second, a fisheye lens does not increase the size and the weakness (in the sense of the complete scene is visible, without loss of information due to dead areas) of the imaging system with respect to a conventional camera. In this case, as shown in Fig. 2.5, the projection model consists of a projection onto a virtual unitary sphere, followed by a perspective projection onto an image plane.

Therefore, the image generated in both cases is different as depicted in Fig. 2.6. Perspective cameras obtained a rectangular image that, in most practical situations, accurately satisfies the extrinsic perspective assumptions. So, for each pixel, the set of $3D$ points projecting to the pixel (i.e., whose possibly-blurred images are centred on the pixel) is a straight line in $3D$ space, and all the light rays meet at a single $3D$ point (the optical centre). On the contrary, fisheye cameras capture circular images such that objects close to the focal point are clear and distinguishable to the user, while the level of detail decreases as objects move further away from the point of

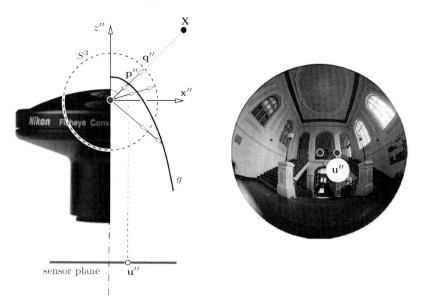

Fig. 2.5 The mapping of a scene point **X** into a sensor plane to a point **u"** for a fisheye lens (courtesy of Mičušík [7])

Fig. 2.6 Sample images captured at the same position by a perspective camera (*left*) and a fisheye camera (*right*)

interest. Thus, the fisheye strategy magnifies the area of interest (located in the focal point) to show the detail, whereas the context is maintained by preserving continuity at the periphery. As a consequence, image distribution is not homogeneous in terms of resolution.

The key concept is to divide an image into the proper regions such that the resulting subimages keep the features of the original images, specially in terms of resolution distribution. So, rectangular regions are described for perspective images, where resolution is approximately uniform along the whole image while a fisheye image is divided into sector portions (see Fig. 2.7). Note that circular regions are not used, even though resolution is laid out in that way. It is because a circular region would cover a 180° 3D area and the neighborhood similarity could not be exploited.

(a)   (b)

Fig. 2.7 Example of image division depending on the kind of camera used

Once the shape of the image regions is determined, a new issue arises: their size. This parameter is important in terms of noise influence as well as uniformity in illumination and gray level. It mainly depends on the position of the camera with respect to the scene such that when the further a camera is, the smaller regions have to be defined. This is because the size of scene elements is proportional to the distance between the camera and those elements.

Note that each region should be identified by a unique value that allows to properly choose the threshold. In particular, statistic functions are commonly used. The statistic which is the most appropriate, largely depends on the input image, although simple and fast functions include the mean, median, or mean of minimum and maximum values of the local intensity distribution. In our case, we have used the mean value to describe each image region.

The next step is to determine the proper CoD techniques to achieve our goal, i.e., an accurate segmentation. As depicted in Fig. 2.8 and sketched in Algorithm 2, different situations have been studied:

1. *The ideal case.* The reference frame for the *background(-frame) subtraction* is free of foreground objects. Thus, three different situations could be faced by the *adjacent frame differencing*:

   - There are no foreground objects in the previous frame. In this case, pixels are classified as foreground when both the *adjacent difference* and the *background(-frame) subtraction* are greater than or equal to their corresponding thresholds
   - A foreground object appears in the previous frame. So, one or both of the *adjacent difference* drawbacks can occur. The *ghosting* problem is solved by taking into account that the *background(-frame) subtraction* does not identify those pixels as foreground. With regard to the *foreground aperture* drawback, it will be solved as follows. When the foreground objects have a similar texture, they are correctly identify by the *background(-frame) subtraction*, but not by

the *adjacent difference*. The way we have solved this situation is considering what makes a pixel be in this situation. Therefore, on the one hand, they must satisfy a gray-level similarity relationship because they belong to the same homogeneous texture. And, on the other hand, the other requirement refers to those pixels that are classified as a foreground object in the previous frame. So, it is necessary to use both constraints to obtain a successful result since whether the similarity criterion was only used, many false alarms could be generated

- The last case takes place when a foreground object stops moving. Again, this situation has been solved by means of a similarity criterion

2. *The general case.* Any foreground object appears in the reference frame. The difference between this case and the previous one is that an element initially considered as a background element can become foreground at any time. Thus, when it starts moving, it leaves behind a *hole* which will be wrongly classified as foreground. Taking advantage of this knowledge, a new method to detect and solve this situation has been designed. Mainly, it consists of a comparison between the segmentation results of the current frame and the content of that blob in the reference frame. Each time a blob results from a *background* element movement, it has been identified that a *hole* should be removed. So, those pixels are now reclassified as background and background frame is updated with the new information. Again, performance in the different conditions considered in the ideal case was also analyzed by using similar solutions for them (see Fig. 2.8).

Note that color images have been used as input in the examples depicted in Fig. 2.8. However, with the aim of obtaining a general solution that is able to run over both color and gray-level images, a preprocessing takes place. Basically, this preprocessing consists of obtaining a gray-level image composed of the intensity channel in the Hue-Saturation-Intensity (HSI) system. Despite other color spaces are available such as, for instance, *Lab*, *YUV*, *XYZ*, etc. HSI is used because it encodes color information by separating an overall intensity value I from two values encoding 'chromaticity'—hue H and saturation S—(see Appendix A for further information). This might also provide better support for computer vision algorithms because it can normalize small lighting changes and focus on the two chromaticity parameters that are more associated with the intrinsic character of a surface rather than the source that is lightning it. In addition, with the purpose of reducing lighting influence on the algorithm's performance, a difference normalization is carried out. Mathematically, it can be expressed as follows:

$$\left| \left(\frac{\sigma_P^2}{\sigma_C^2} * (Ngray_C - \mu_C) \right) - Ngray_P \right| \qquad (2.3)$$

where the indexes C and P, respectively, correspond to current and previous (reference image in case of the *background subtraction*) frame; $Ngray$ represents the gray level for the considered pixel, while σ^2 and μ, respectively, refer to the standard deviation and the average of the image intensities.

In addition, take into account that two consecutive morphological operations are applied on the binary image resulting from the segmentation process in order to suppress small errors in the background/foreground classification method. So, first, a 3×3 erode filter is used to erase isolated points or lines caused by different dynamic factors such as sensor noise, non-uniform attenuation, or blinking of the lights. Then, a foreground region recovery is achieved by means of a 3×3 expand filter. It is specially useful when two different parts of the same interest object appear divided due to capture and/or segmentation errors.

Another important issue is sudden, global changes in illumination. A common way to solve this situation consists of generating an alarm when a considerable part of the image (usually two thirds of the image) has changed, that is, has been classified as foreground. Although it works well in most cases, it fails when that change is due to target's proximity to the camera. This situation has been solved by comparing the amount of foreground pixels detected in the current frame and in the previous one. So, it is assumed that a global illumination has occurred when more than two-thirds of the image are classified as foreground and the amount of foreground pixels detected in the current frame is greater than 1.5 times the amount detected in the previous frame. Note that this kind of illumination change makes necessary to set a new reference frame for the *background(-frame) subtraction* technique. Moreover,

---

Algorithm 2 Combination of Differences **(CoD)**

```
for each pixel x do
  if (|F_t(x) − B(x)| ≥ τ_B(x)) then
    if (|F_t(x) − F_{t−1}(x)| ≥ τ_A(x)) then
      Foreground Pixel;
    else if ((|F_t(x) − F_{t−1}(x)| < τ_S) AND (Foreground(F_{t−1}(x)))) then
      Foreground Pixel; // Foreground Aperture
    else
      Background Pixel;
    end if
  else if ((|F_t(x) − F_{t−1}(x)| ≥ τ_A(x)) AND (|F_t(x) − B(x)| < τ_B(x))) then
    Background Pixel; // Ghosting problem
  else
    Background Pixel;
  end if
end for
Collect pixels in blobs;
for each pixel x do
  if (Foreground(F_{t−1}(x))) then
    if (NO (|F_t(x) − F_{t−1}(x)| < τ_S)) then
      Pixel Re-classification (From Foreground to Background); //It is a hole
      Update background reference frame
    end if
  end if
end for
```

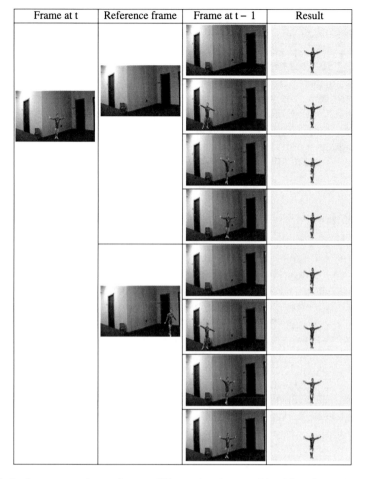

Frame at t	Reference frame	Frame at t − 1	Result

Fig. 2.8 Performance result samples over different situations considered in order to determine the proper combination of difference techniques for an accurate segmentation

some lighting sources require several milliseconds to stabilize. For that reason, when a global illumination change has been detected, the system waits for some frames (typically five frames in our experiments) before resetting all its parameters.

2.3 Experimental Results

In this section, we evaluate the performance of the proposed segmentation procedure. For that, two different kind of experiments have been carried out. First, the CoD's performance is assessed by using the video images provided by three different image datasets in the literature: the Wallflower Dataset [8], the image dataset developed for the Forth ACM International Workshop on Video Surveillance & Sensor Networks (VSSN06) [9], and the Audiovisual People Dataset, courtesy of Engineering and Physical Sciences Research Council funded MOTINAS project (EP/D033772/1) [10]. Although there exist other datasets such as, for instance, PETS 2006 Benchmark Data [11], to name any, they have not been used here since they aim at a different goal such as the identification of an unattended luggage. Finally, the results over our own dataset composed of both perspective and fisheye images are presented. Note that the qualitative results are displayed as binary images where pixels of interest are coded by the white color, while the background is identified by the black color.

2.3.1 Principles for Performance Evaluation and Comparison

The performance of a motion segmentation technique can be evaluated visually and quantitatively based on the task requirements. So, on the one hand, a qualitative/visual evaluation can be achieved by displaying a flicker animation [12] or a short movie file containing a registered pair of images that are played in fast succession at intervals of about a second each, among others. In that way, in the absence of change, one perceives a steady image, while when changes are present, the changed regions appear to flicker. The estimated change mask can be also superimposed on each image (e.g., as a semitransparent overlay, with different colors for different types of change).

On the other hand, a quantitative evaluation is more challenging. First, because of the difficulty of establishing a valid ground truth, that is, the process of defining the *correct answer* for what *exactly* the algorithm is expected to produce. Arriving at the ground truth is an image analysis that is known to be difficult and time-consuming [13], since it is usually done by human beings and the same human observer can generate different segmentations for the same data at two different times. A secondary issue is to define the relative importance of the different types of errors. There are several standard methods for comparing the ground truth to a candidate binary change mask. The following amounts are generally involved:

- True positives (TP): the number of foreground pixels correctly detected
- False positives (FP): the average of false alarms per frame, i.e., the number of background pixels incorrectly detected as foreground
- True negatives (TN): the number of background pixels correctly detected
- False negatives (FN): the average of false misses, that is, the number of foreground pixels incorrectly detected as background.

From them, Rosin and Ioannidis [14] described three methods for quantifying method's performance:

- *The Percentage Correct Classification (PCC)*, also called *accuracy*, is used as a statistical measurement of how well the segmentation process identifies or excludes foreground pixels. Mathematically, it can be expressed as follows:

$$PCC = \frac{TP + TN}{TP + FP + TN + FN} \tag{2.4}$$

So, an accuracy of 100 % means that the measured values are exactly the same as the given values in the ground truth.

- The Jaccard coefficient (JC) is a statistic used for comparing the similarity and diversity of sample sets and is defined as:

$$JC = \frac{TP}{TP + FP + FN} \tag{2.5}$$

- The Yule coefficient (YC) is a statistic summarizing the extent to which two variables are independent or not, as in the case of the correlation coefficient. It is obtained as follows:

$$YC = \left| \frac{TP}{TP + FP} + \frac{TN}{TN + FN} - 1 \right| \tag{2.6}$$

On the contrary, other authors quantify how well an algorithm matches the ground truth by means of *recall* and *precision* measurements [15, 16]. Thus, *recall* (also known as true positive rate (TPR) or *sensitivity*) [17] is computed as the ratio of the number of foreground pixels correctly identified to the number of foreground pixels in the ground truth; whereas precision or positive predictive value (PPV) is obtained as the ratio of the number of foreground pixels properly identified to the number of foreground pixels detected. That is:

$$Recall = TPR = \frac{\sharp \text{ of foreground pixels correctly detected}}{\text{total } \sharp \text{ of ground-truth foreground pixels}} = \frac{TP}{TP + FN} \tag{2.7}$$

$$Precision = PPV = \frac{\sharp \text{ of foreground pixels correctly detected}}{\text{total } \sharp \text{ of foreground pixels detected}} = \frac{TP}{TP + FP} \tag{2.8}$$

Other metrics which can be used are:

- False Positive Rate (FPR) which measures background pixels misclassified as foreground such that:

$$FPR = \frac{FP}{(FP + TN)} \tag{2.9}$$

- False Negative Rate (FNR) that refers to foreground pixels erroneously tagged as background. Similar to the previous measurement, it is defined as follows:

$$FNR = \frac{FN}{(FN + TP)} \tag{2.10}$$

- Specificity (SPC) or True Negative Rate (TNR) which expresses the ratio of detected foreground pixels that are true positives. Thus, a specificity of 100 % means that the segmentation process recognizes all actual negatives, that is, 100 % specificity means no positives are erroneously tagged. In a more formal way:

$$SPC = \frac{TN}{(FP + TN)} = 1 - FPR \qquad (2.11)$$

- *Negative Predictive Value (NPV)* that quantifies the ratio of background pixels correctly identified. Its value is obtained as:

$$NPV = \frac{TN}{(TN + FN)} \qquad (2.12)$$

- *False Discovery Rate (FDR)* or *False Alarm Rate (FAR)* which measures the foreground pixels misclassified as background:

$$FDR = FAR = \frac{FP}{(FP + TP)} \qquad (2.13)$$

- *Mathews Correlation Coefficient (MCC)* that is used as a measurement of the quality of binary classifications. That is, MCC is, in essence, a correlation coefficient between the observed and the predicted binary classifications. Actually, it takes into account true and false positives and is generally regarded as a balanced measurement. Its value oscillates between -1 and 1 such that a coefficient of 1 represents a perfect prediction, 0 an average random prediction, and -1 an inverse prediction. Mathematically, it is defined as follows:

$$MCC = \frac{(TP * TN) - (FP * FN)}{\sqrt{(TP + FN) * (TP + FP) * (FN + TP) * (FN + TN)}} \qquad (2.14)$$

Note that if any of the four sums in the denominator is zero, the denominator will be arbitrarily set to 1; this results in a Mathews correlation coefficient of zero, which can be shown to be the correct limiting value

- F_1 *score* which is a measurement of a process' accuracy. It considers both precision and recall of the test to compute the score as follows:

$$F_1 = 2 * \frac{precision * recall}{precision + recall} \qquad (2.15)$$

The F_1 score can be interpreted as a weighted average of the precision and recall, where an F_1 score reaches its best value at 1 and the worst score at 0

Table 2.1 Parameter values used for evaluating the **CoD** performance over the three considered image datasets

Subimage Size	10x10
Nframes for Initial Background Model	200
Erosion Mask	0 1 0 / 0 1 1 / 0 0 0
Dilation Mask	1 1 1 / 1 1 1 / 1 1 1

2.3.2 Experimental Results Over Image Datasets

In this section, three different image datasets are used to evaluate CoD's performance. For that, the set of parameters, listed in Table 2.1, has been the same over all of the considered image sequences.

2.3.2.1 Wallflower Dataset

This dataset was created to evaluate background modeling algorithms from the definition of ten canonical problems that an ideal background maintenance system should overcome:

- *Moved objects.* When a background object is moved, it should not be considered as foreground
- *Time of day*: The passage of time generates gradual illumination changes that alter the background appearance
- *Light switch.* Sudden changes in illumination such as switching on/off lights or opening/closing a window modify the background appearance
- *Bootstrap.* A frame without foreground objects is not available in some environments
- *Foreground Aperture.* When the entire target does not appear as foreground because it is homogeneously colored and the change in the interior pixels cannot be detected
- *Waving trees.* Some background elements can vacillate (e.g., swaying branches, blinking of screens, etc) by requiring models which can represent those disjoint sets of pixel values
- *Camouflage.* Foreground object's pixel characteristics can be subsumed by the modeled background
- *Sleeping person.* The distinction between a foreground object that becomes motionless and a background object that moves and then becomes motionless
- *Waking person.* When an object initially in the background moves, both it and the newly revealed parts of the background appear to change

- *Shadows*. The foreground objects often cast shadows which appear different from the modeled background.

However, only seven real video sequences, with a test image and its corresponding ground truth, are included in this dataset by presenting typical critical situations. All of the test sequences were taken with a 3-CCD camera recording to digital tape at a size of 160×120 pixels, sampled at 4 Hz. Nevertheless, in this section, we have only used those video sequences corresponding to the case under study, that is, those with a static background. Therefore, the used video sequences are: *Time-of-day*, *Light-switch*, *Bootstrap*, and *Foreground-aperture*.

With the aim for evaluating the performance of our approach, it is qualitative and quantitative compared with previous algorithms that have provided results over this dataset. Those approaches can be briefly summarized as follows:

- *Mixture of Gaussians* [18]. A pixel-wise mixture of three Gaussians models the background. Each Gaussian is weighted according to the frequency with which it explains the observed background ($\pm 2\sigma$). The most heavily weighted Gaussians that together explain over 50 % of past data are considered background
- *Normalized Block Correlation* [19]. Images are split into blocks. The pixels in each block are represented as their respective medians over the training images. Each block is represented as its median template and the standard deviation of the block-wise normalized correlation from the median over the training images. For each incoming block, normalized correlation values that deviate too much from the expected deviations cause the block to be considered foreground
- *Temporal Derivative* [20]. In the training phase, for each pixel, the minimum and maximum values are saved along with the maximum interframe change in intensity. Any pixel that deviates from its minimum or maximum by more than the maximum interframe change is considered foreground. They additionally enforced a minimum interframe difference of 10 pixels after the regular training phase
- *Bayesian Decision* [21]. Pixel value probability densities, represented as normalized histograms, are accumulated over time, and backgrounds are determined by a straightforward maximum *a posteriori* criterion
- *Eigenbackground* [22]. Images of motionless backgrounds are collected. Principle Component Analysis (PCA) is used to determine means and variances over the entire sequence (whole images as vectors). So, the incoming images are projected onto the PCA subspace. The differences between the projection and the current image greater than a threshold are considered foreground
- *Wallflower* [23]. Images are processed at three different spatial scales:
  - pixel level, which makes the preliminary classification foreground-background as well as the adaptation to changing backgrounds
  - region level that refines the raw classification of the pixel level based on inter-pixel relationships
  - frame level, designed for dealing with the light switch problem

- *Tracey LAB LP* [24]. The background is represented by a set of codebook vectors locally modeling the background intensities in the spatial-range domain. Thus, the image pixels not fitting that set are classified as foreground. In addition, as in the *Wallflower* algorithm, a frame-level analysis is used to discriminate between global light changes, noise, and objects of interest. Moreover, the foreground is also represented by a set of codebook vectors in order to obtain a more accurate foreground segmentation. Note that images are treated in the *CIE Lab* color space and filtered with a 2×2 mean low-pass filter as preprocessing

- *RGT* [25]. Image processing is carried out at region level, where background is modeled at different scales, from large to small rectangular regions, by using the color histogram and a texture measurement. So, motion is detected by comparing the corresponding rectangular regions from the coarsest scale to the finest one such that the comparisons are done at a finer scale only if motion was detected at a coarser scale. Furthermore, a Gaussian mixture background subtraction in combination with Minimum Difference of Pair Assignments (MDPA) distance [26] is used at the finest scale

- *Joint Difference* [4]. Motion is detected by means of an hybrid technique that uses both frame-by-frame difference and background subtraction. This technique integrates a selective updating method of the background model to tune background adaptation. In addition to a pixel-by-pixel difference in the *RGB* color space, a shadow filter in the *HSV* space is used to improve segmentation process.

A qualitative analysis highlights a good performance of the proposed approach (Fig. 2.9). It is worth noting that both *Time-of-day* and *Foreground-aperture* results present some false positives around the real foreground element due to the criteria designed to detect stop-moving foreground elements. Nevertheless, targets are correctly detected in all images, even though in *Bootstrapping* video sequence, where foreground elements appear from the first frame. This means that our approach successfully deals with the two well-known difference drawbacks (i.e. *ghosting* and *foreground aperture*).

From a quantitative point of view, two different statistical measurements have been considered: TPR and FPR. As previously introduced, the TPR evaluates foreground pixel classification. Thus, a high TPR means that the number of foreground pixels correctly classified is much larger than the number of foreground pixels misclassified as background. Nevertheless, it is also necessary to investigate the influence of the real background pixels in the extracted foreground, since TPR is just about the actual foreground pixels. For that, FPR is used to measure how many background pixels are classified as background. Note that the best technique should have the highest TPR value, but the lowest FPR value because a high FPR value means that most parts of the image are detected as foreground by making the background subtraction technique under study not appropriate to achieve our final goal.

Focusing on the results presented in Fig. 2.10, our approach has the best results except for the *Foreground-aperture* video sequence. The reason is that it has been influenced by the criteria established for detecting the situation when an object stops moving, and they have produced some false positives in the previous location of the target's head. On the other hand, the *FPR* is low (less than 5%) what means most of the image pixels are correctly classified (see Fig. 2.11). So, as the proposed approach

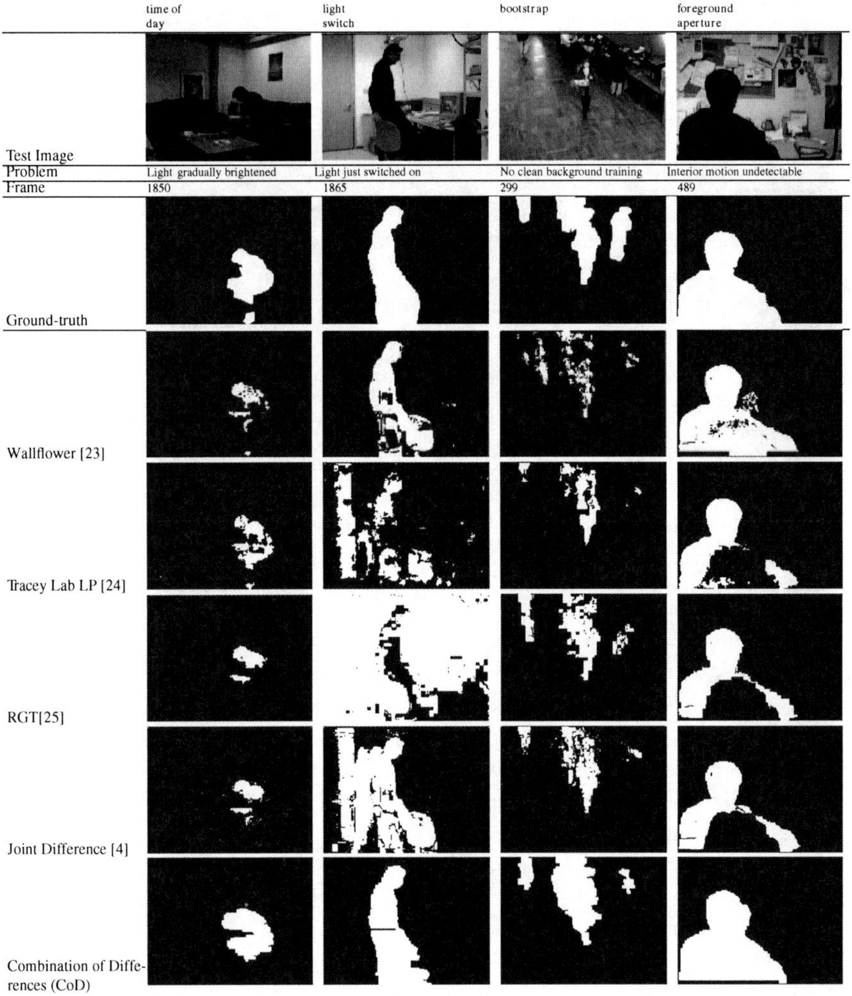

Fig. 2.9 Tests of different background maintenance algorithms for four canonical background problems contained in the *Wallflower* dataset [8] such that each column represents one considered image sequence. The *top row* shows the image in the sequence at which the processing was stopped. The *second row* shows hand-segmented images of the foreground used as *ground truth* for a quantitative comparison. The *rest rows* show the results of one algorithm

combines the highest TPR value and a low FPR value in most of the video sequences, it can be concluded that our segmentation process outperforms previous algorithm results.

Moreover, a quantitative analysis in terms of *recall* and *precision* is presented in Table 2.2. It can be observed that although another algorithm achieves a better result for a measurement in any situation, it is at the cost of obtaining a bad result

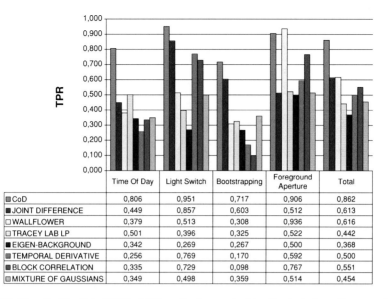

	Time Of Day	Light Switch	Bootstrapping	Foreground Aperture	Total
▨ CoD	0,806	0,951	0,717	0,906	0,862
■ JOINT DIFFERENCE	0,449	0,857	0,603	0,512	0,613
▢ WALLFLOWER	0,379	0,513	0,308	0,936	0,616
▢ TRACEY LAB LP	0,501	0,396	0,325	0,522	0,442
■ EIGEN-BACKGROUND	0,342	0,269	0,267	0,500	0,368
▨ TEMPORAL DERIVATIVE	0,256	0,769	0,170	0,592	0,500
■ BLOCK CORRELATION	0,335	0,729	0,098	0,767	0,551
▨ MIXTURE OF GAUSSIANS	0,349	0,498	0,359	0,514	0,454

Fig. 2.10 True Positive Rate (TPR) of different background subtraction techniques for some video sequences of the *Wallflower* dataset [8], by including an extra column, *Total* that represents the result obtained for all the videos combined together. Note that, as TPR evaluates the foreground pixel classification, a high TPR value means that the number of foreground pixels correctly classified is much larger than the number of foreground pixels misclassified as background

for the other measurement. That is, there is no video sequence for which a previous algorithm overcomes the performance of CoD in both *recall* and *precision*.

A deeper quantitative study reveals the good performance of the proposed approach (see Table 2.3). So, first, TNR which expresses how many positive are wrongly tagged is presented. A high value of this measurement means a more accurate image segmentation since less background pixels were wrongly tagged as foreground. As it can be seen, the obtained results are close to 100 %. Nevertheless, as in the case of FPR, TNR cannot be the only criterion for the evaluation of a segmentation technique. As a complementary measurement, NPV is used for evaluating how many foreground pixels have been wrongly classified as background. Again, a high value of this parameter refers to a more accurate performance. The results are also near 100 %. Moreover, TNR measurement can be complemented with the FDR measurement when we are more interested in evaluating the error rate with respect to misclassified background pixels, that is, the percentage of the background pixels erroneously tagged as foreground. From its definition, a good performance will provide a low value for this parameter. As it can be checked in Table 2.3, FDR is lower than 17 %, except for the *Bootstrap* sequence, which is slightly higher. The reason lies on the continuous presence of foreground elements in some parts of the image. This fact makes more difficult the segmentation problem.

On the other hand, the following measurements provide a global evaluation for the algorithm's performance. The first considered one is *accuracy* since it takes

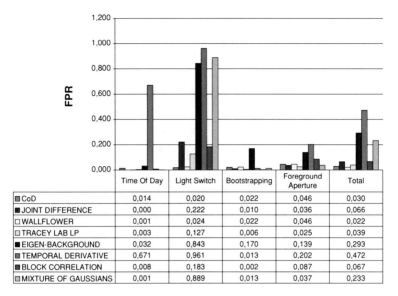

	Time Of Day	Light Switch	Bootstrapping	Foreground Aperture	Total
▣ CoD	0,014	0,020	0,022	0,046	0,030
◼ JOINT DIFFERENCE	0,000	0,222	0,010	0,036	0,066
☐ WALLFLOWER	0,001	0,024	0,022	0,046	0,022
☐ TRACEY LAB LP	0,003	0,127	0,006	0,025	0,039
◼ EIGEN-BACKGROUND	0,032	0,843	0,170	0,139	0,293
▨ TEMPORAL DERIVATIVE	0,671	0,961	0,013	0,202	0,472
◼ BLOCK CORRELATION	0,008	0,183	0,002	0,087	0,067
▨ MIXTURE OF GAUSSIANS	0,001	0,889	0,013	0,037	0,233

Fig. 2.11 False Positive Rate (FPR) of different background subtraction techniques for some video sequences of the *Wallflower* dataset [8], by including an additional column, *Total*, which contains the FPR for all the videos combined together. FPR is used to measuring how many background pixels are classified as background. Therefore, the best segmentation technique will have the lowest FPR value

into account pixels both correctly and wrongly classified. Mathematically speaking, *accuracy* will be higher when lower classification errors are made. Thus, an *accuracy* of 100 % is desired. The obtained results are >90 % in all the considered image sequences. Another way to assess the system's performance is based on the MCC value. Basically, it is a balance measurement that provides information about the correlation between pixels correctly tagged and those wrongly classified. So, values near 1, as the ones obtained for the proposed approach, result in an accurate segmentation. Note that a lower value is again obtained for the *Bootstrap* sequence. The reason is the continuous presence of foreground elements in some parts of the image. Regarding F_1 *Score*, it is a kind of average of *precision* and *recall* measurements. The F_1 *Score* reaches its best value at 1. Note that all the obtained results are close to the unit. The JC evaluates the algorithm's accuracy when foreground pixels are considered. So, a low error rate will provide JC values around 1. In this case, the *Bootstrap* and the *Time-of-day* sequences have obtained the lowest values. Finally, the YC value expresses the relationship between foreground and background pixels correctly tagged and its value oscillates between 1 and −1, by providing a better performance when it is around 1. All values are positive and close to the unit. Again, the *Bootstrap* sequence has obtained the worst result, although it is nearly 0.70.

Table 2.2 Comparison of the experimental quantitative results, in terms of *recall* and *precision*, obtained for different segmentation methods on some *Wallflower* benchmarks [8]

Algorithm	Measurement	Time of day	Light switch	Bootstrap	Foreground aperture	Total
Mixture of Gaussians	recall	34.88	49.82	35.93	51.37	45.43
[18]	precision	96.43	10.27	82.89	82.96	27.94
Block corre-lation	recall	33.46	72.86	9.81	76.66	55.11
[19]	precision	79.33	44.82	89.13	75.79	61.93
Temporal derivative	recall	25.65	76.89	16.99	59.20	49.96
[20]	precision	20.26	17.44	13.21	93.20	17.39
Bayesian decision	recall	34.24	26.86	26.74	50.00	36.84
[21]	precision	48.53	6.11	22.05	55.97	20.04
Eigenback ground	recall	43.22	70.44	89.61	51.39	64.03
[22]	precision	97.66	86.36	29.95	82.78	53.68
Wallflower	recall	37.92	51.29	30.77	93.63	61.64
[23]	precision	95.92	81.65	71.15	87.87	84.75
Tracey LAB LP	recall	50.13	39.61	32.51	52.15	44.20
[24]	precision	93.49	38.91	91.18	88.03	69.05
RGT	recall	29.09	51.19	57.76	50.18	47.06
[25]						
Joint difference	recall	44.90	85.68	60.34	51.20	61.13
[4]	precision	99.00	44.04	91.40	83.34	64.89
Combination of	recall	80.62	95.11	71.69	90.56	**86.19**
differences	precision	83.31	90.82	73.73	88.55	**85.27**

2.3.2.2 VSSN06 Dataset

This dataset was developed for an algorithm competition in Foreground/Background Segmentation within the *Forth ACM International Workshop on Video Surveillance and Sensor Networks*. Their motivation was based on the results reported in the literature that did not provide a direct comparison among algorithms because each

Table 2.3 Quantitative results obtained for the **CoD** approach over some video sequences of the *Wallflower* dataset [8] such that the first three measurements (TNR, NPV, and FDR) provide a performance evaluation related to misclassified/correctly classified pixels, while the rest of measurements provide a global assessment of the algorithm performance

	Time of day	Light switch	Bootstrap	Foreground aperture	Total
TNR	98.58	98.04	95.41	95.85	97.04
NPV	98.31	98.99	94.94	96.63	97.24
FDR	16.69	9.18	26.27	11.45	14.73
Accuracy	97.14	97.54	91.80	94.45	95.24
MCC	0.80	0.91	0.68	0.86	0.83
F_1 Score	0.82	0.93	0.73	0.90	0.86
JC	0.69	0.87	0.57	0.81	0.75
YC	0.82	0.90	0.69	0.85	0.83

So, high values for TNR, NPV, accuracy, MCC, F_1 score, JC, and YC, and low values of FDR result in an accurate segmentation

researcher reports results using different assumptions, evaluation methods, and test sequences.

Each of its 12 test videos consists of a video that illustrates a background with dynamic elements sometimes, and one or more virtual foreground objects, taken from [27, 28] together with a foreground mask video (ground-truth video), in most of the video sequences, by specifying each pixel belonging to a foreground object. These color videos evaluate algorithm's performance in view of the different canonical problems mentioned above. Particularly, the considered problems here are:

• oscillating background
• gradual illumination changes
• sudden changes in illumination
• bootstrapping
• shadows

Again, we have concentrated on those video sequences that evaluate algorithm's performance when background elements are motionless. Therefore, only four videos are considered. So, in *video sequence 1*, an indoor scene without oscillating elements is the background where a virtual girl is moving around. No ground truth information has been provided for this video sequence. That is why only qualitative results are presented. So, as it can be observed in Fig. 2.12, the target element was detected in all frames, even when the target is partially visible (e.g. frame at time 143). However, some false positives appear around the foreground object. That is because the similarity criterion is defined at pixel level and no extra information is used. Therefore, a more accurate segmentation could be obtained if any cognitive knowledge is integrated in the system.

In a similar way, the *video sequence 2* represents an indoor scene where no oscillating elements appear. In this case, the target elements are two boys who are dancing along the whole scene. Again, the qualitative results, presented in Fig. 2.13, highlight the proper identification of the background and foreground pixels. As in the

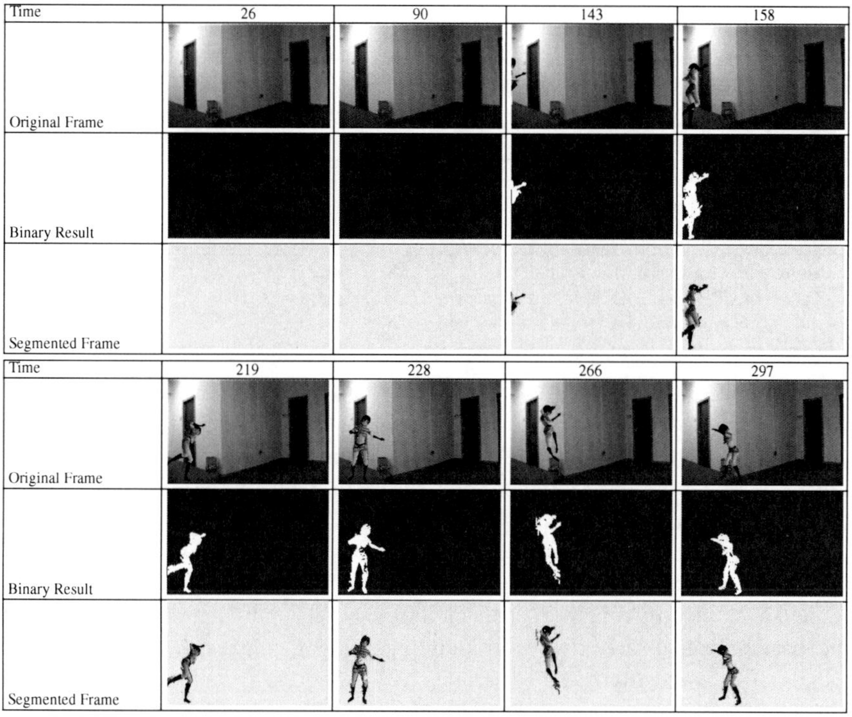

4

Fig. 2.12 Qualitative results for the *video sequence 1* of the *VSSN06* dataset [9], where a virtual girl is moving around an indoor scene without oscillating elements. So, the *first row* of each block shows the original frame of the sequence, while the *other rows* depict the segmentation result obtained by the **CoD** approach: a binary image representing the background/foreground classification carried out, such that the background is represented by *black color* and the foreground pixels are coded in *white*; and a color image, where the foreground elements appear as in the original frame, whereas the background is coded in an artificial, homogeneous color

previous case, a few false alarms have been detected in the surrounding target borders. Nevertheless, the quantitative results reflect the good performance of the algorithm with high values for measurements corresponding to correctly tagged pixels, whereas those related to misclassified pixels have low values (see Table 2.4).

With regard to the *video sequence 5*, as in *video sequences 1* and *2*, a static indoor scene is used as background. The particularity of this sequence is the presence of foreground elements from the first frame. In addition, two different kinds of target elements are considered. On the one hand, a virtual human being who is dancing around the scene. On the other hand, a cat which is walking around the scene. Thus, this video sequence evaluates both the presence of foreground elements during the whole experiment and the detection of target elements different from human beings. As depicted in Fig. 2.14, both elements of interest were successfully identified. It is worth noting that the presence of a foreground element in the reference frame has been properly detected when it started to move by solving the *ghosting*

Table 2.4 Quantitative results obtained for the **CoD** approach over some video sequences of the *VSSN06* dataset [9] such that the first seven measurements provide a performance evaluation related to misclassified/correctly classified pixels, while the rest of measurements provide a global assessment

	Recall	Precision	TPR	FPR	TNR	NPV	FDR	Accuracy	MCC	F_1 Score	JC	YC
Video 2	80.07	86.25	80.07	0.39	99.61	99.43	13.75	99.09	0.82	0.82	0.70	0.86
Video 5	79.22	73.90	73.90	2.86	97.14	98.73	25.02	96.18	0.73	0.73	0.60	0.70
Video 6	71.71	87.81	71.17	0.81	99.19	97.92	10.85	97.29	0.77	0.76	0.65	0.83

So, high values for recall, precision, TPR, TNR, NPV, accuracy, MCC, F_1 score, JC and YC, and low values of FPR and FDR, result in an accurate segmentation

problem. Nevertheless, the no detection of the foreground element in the early frames has influenced the quantitative results, summarized in Table 2.4. So, although the relationship between the measurements to show a good performance is kept, the values are a little bit lower, or higher in the case of the pixel misclassification, than it could be expected.

Again, the problem of lacking a frame free of foreground elements is considered in the *video sequence 6*. The background scene is similar to the one in *video sequences 1, 2* and *5*, an indoor scene with constant illumination conditions where one or more foreground elements are moving around. In particular, a virtual boy is in the scene in the first captured frame, moves around, leaves, and re-enters the scene, while a little girl enters and leaves the scene during the whole experiment. Both qualitative and quantitative results are presented (see Fig. 2.15 and Table 2.4). Analyzing the qualitative results, the foreground element is not detected in the early frames, since it is not moving and it is initially classified as background. Then, it starts moving and the proposed approach has detected this situation by properly updating its reference frame. That is why there is no *ghost* presence in the frame at time 21. Later, the girl enters the scene and both targets are detected without any problem, even when they partially appear, as in frame at time 367 or at time 380. From a quantitative point of view, bootstrapping event has had less influence on the results than on the previous video sequence by showing a better performance, i.e., a lower error rate.

2.3.2.3 Audiovisual People Dataset

This dataset, courtesy of EPSRC funded MOTINAS project (EP/D033772/1), for uni-modal and multi-modal (audio and visual) people detection tracking, consists of three video sequences recorded in different scenarios with a video camera and two microphones, although, in our case, only the image sequences have been used.

The 8-bit color AVI sequences were recorded by using a KOBI KF-31CD analog CCD surveillance camera in the Department of Electronic Engineering—Queen Mary University of London. Two of the image sequences were recorded in rooms with reverberations, whereas the third one was recorded in a room with reduced

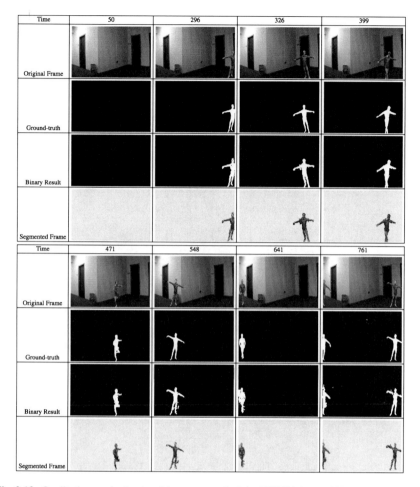

Fig. 2.13 Qualitative results for the *video sequence 2* of the *VSSN06* dataset [9], where two virtual boys are dancing along an indoor scene where no oscillating elements appear. So, the *first row* shows the original frame of the sequence, the *second row* depicts the ground truth frame and, the last *two rows* illustrate the segmentation result obtained by the **CoD** approach: a binary image representing the background/foreground classification carried out, such that the background is represented by *black color* and the foreground pixels are coded in *white*; and a color image, where the foreground elements appear as in the original frame, whereas the background is coded in an artificial, homogeneous color

reverberations, although all of them were captured at a frame rate of 25 Hz with a 360×288 resolution.

Unlike the previous study cases, no quantitative results are presented since no ground truth is provided for this dataset. However, it is used because it considers some issues that are missed in the previous datasets such as occlusions, the change in targets' speed, and/or in the camera pose with respect to the scene.

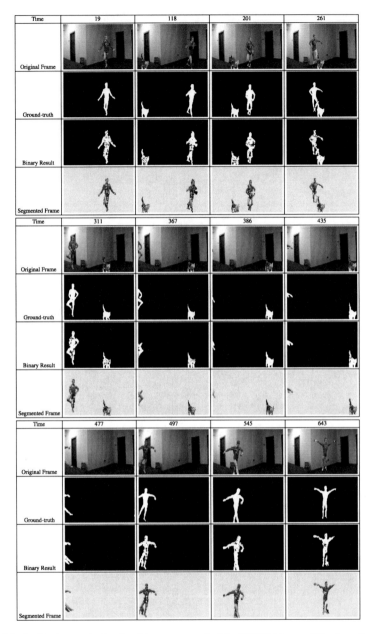

Fig. 2.14 Qualitative results for the *video sequence 5* of the *VSSN06* dataset [9], where the lack of frames without foreground elements is analyzed. So, the *first row* shows the original frame of the sequence, the *second row* depicts the ground truth frame and, the last *two rows* illustrate the segmentation result obtained by the **CoD** approach: a binary image representing the background/foreground classification carried out, such that the background is represented by *black color* and the foreground pixels are coded in *white*; and a color image, where the foreground elements appear as in the original frame, whereas the background is coded in an artificial, homogeneous color

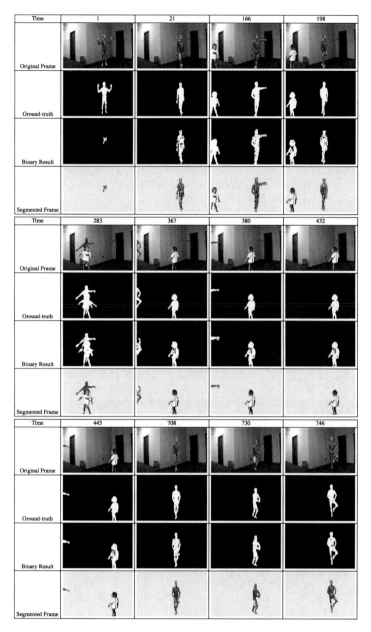

Fig. 2.15 Qualitative results for the *video sequence 6* of the *VSSN06* dataset [9] such that the problem of the absence of a frame free of foreground elements is studied. So, the *first row* shows the original frame of the sequence, the *second row* depicts the ground-truth frame and, the last *two rows* illustrate the segmentation result obtained by the **CoD** approach: a binary image representing the background/foreground classification carried out, such that the background is represented by *black color* and the foreground pixels are coded in *white*; and a color image, where the foreground elements appear as in the original frame, whereas the background is coded in an artificial, homogeneous color

At first instance, a classroom where a person is moving around is observed. Again, the problem of the foreground element presence in the initial frames and its corresponding presence in the reference frame for the *background(-frame) subtraction* is considered. Moreover, in this video sequence, the occlusion problem is also taken into account. So, the target of the sequence, a guy, appears on the left of the image in the initial frames and, while he is moving toward the right side, is occluded. Then, he reappears in the scene and walks around it by approaching and going away until he again disappears of the image as a consequence of a new occlusion. Finally, he re-enters the scene and moves around it. Figure 2.16 shows some frame samples of the obtained result. It is worth noting that the person of interest was successfully detected in all the frames although he was occluded and his distance with respect to the camera was considerable and variable.

In a similar way, the second considered video sequence observes a computer room where two people are constantly entering and leaving it. Nevertheless, in this case, the initial frames are free of foreground pixels which means that the reference frame for the *background(-frame) subtraction*, initially set to the first captured frame, is an exact model of scene background. So, the interest in this video sequence lies on the number of targets, i.e., two individuals, and the fact that they are crossing and overlapping several times during the whole experiment. In the resulting frames, depicted in Fig. 2.17, different situations are analyzed: (1) the absence of foreground elements; (2) the partial presence and subsequent appearance of one of the interest people; (3) the presence of one or both of them, even when they cross (e.g. frame at time 810); and, (4) the scene without any foreground element. Again, from a qualitative point of view, the proposed approach presents a good performance.

The last video sequence was recorded in a room with reduced reverberations. Basically, there are two people who continuously enter and leave the scene such that they change their speed and trajectories all the time. As it can be observed in Fig. 2.18, the individuals are properly detected in all frames. Note the presence of shadows in some of the resulting images, since no processing to erase them has been applied at this point.

2.3.3 Experimental Results Over Our Own Dataset

In this section, we present some results obtained from different experiments carried out in our laboratory. Mainly, they consist of locating an imaging device at different places of our laboratory room. Although the lab contains some dynamic factors (e.g., blinking of computer screens), they have been avoided for this section. Furthermore, as previously pointed out, two different kinds of imaging devices have been used. So, results for both perspective and fisheye devices are presented.

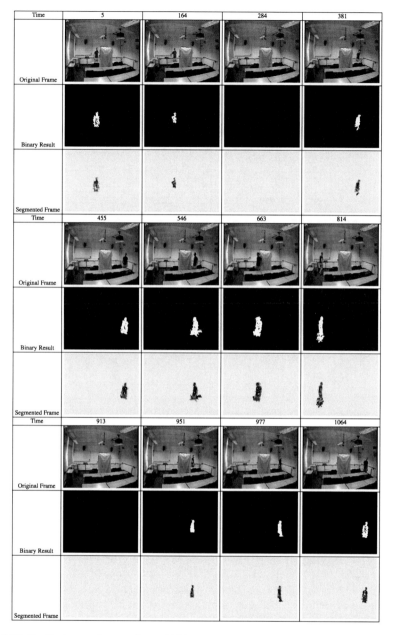

Fig. 2.16 Qualitative results over *Room 105* image sequence of Audiovisual People dataset [10] where a person is moving around a classroom. So, the *first row* of each block shows the original frame of the sequence, whereas the last *two rows* illustrate the segmentation result obtained by the **CoD** approach: a binary image representing the background/foreground classification carried out, such that the background is represented by *black color* and the foreground pixels are coded in *white*; and a color image, where the foreground elements appear as in the original frame, whereas the background is coded in an artificial, homogeneous color

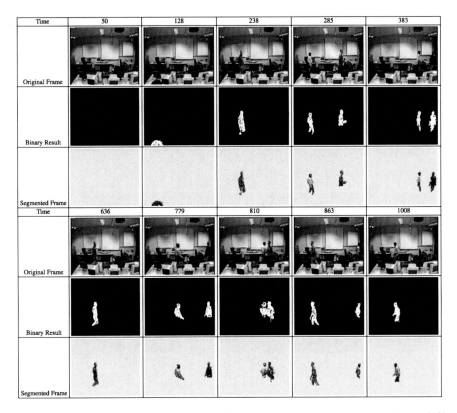

Fig. 2.17 Qualitative results over *Room 160* video sequence of Audiovisual People dataset [10] where two people are moving around a computer room. So, the *first row* of each group shows the original frame of the sequence, whereas the last *two rows* illustrate the segmentation result obtained by the **CoD** approach: a binary image representing the background/foreground classification carried out, such that the background is represented by *black color* and the foreground pixels are coded in *white*; and a color image, where the foreground elements appear as in the original frame, whereas the background is coded in an artificial, homogeneous color

2.3.3.1 Perspective Image Experiments

First, a perspective imaging device has been used. In particular, a *STH-DCSG Stereo head* by using one of its two C-mount lenses was employed [29]. Basically, it is a synchronized digital stereo head camera with two global shutter CMOS imagers, offering VGA resolutions at 30 fps. Nevertheless, different features have been tested. So, on the one hand, images were acquired in *monochrome* mode with a 320×240 resolution and, on the other hand, 640×480, 24-bit RGB color images are considered.

In both experiments, the goal is to properly detect the presence of a person in the scene, continuously entering and leaving the observed space. However, experimental conditions have been changed. In the first experiment, illumination changes do not occur. An individual enters and moves around the scene by approaching and moving

Fig. 2.18 Qualitative results over *Chamber* video sequence of Audiovisual People dataset [10] where two people are continuously entering and leaving a room with reduced reverberations. So, the *first row* of each group shows the original frame of the sequence, whereas the last *two rows* illustrate the segmentation result obtained by the **CoD** approach: a binary image representing the background/foreground classification carried out, such that the background is represented by *black color* and the foreground pixels are coded in *white*; and a color image, where the foreground elements appear as in the original frame, whereas the background is coded in an artificial, homogeneous color

away the camera until a distance of 9 m. Furthermore, occlusions and stop motions have been also analyzed with this image sequence. A good performance is obtained in all those situations as depicted in Fig. 2.19.

Regarding the second experiment, the camera was located at a different place in our laboratory room. Again, a person is continuously entering, moving around, and leaving the scene. However, in this case, global illumination changes take place. So, initially, the visual system is observing a very bright scene. As shown in the first row of Fig. 2.20, the target individual is successfully detected at several positions, in spite of some internal pixels are misclassified as background. The main reason lies on the similarity between the pixel intensities since CoD algorithm works at pixel level. Then, a global illumination change takes place by slightly darkening the scene.

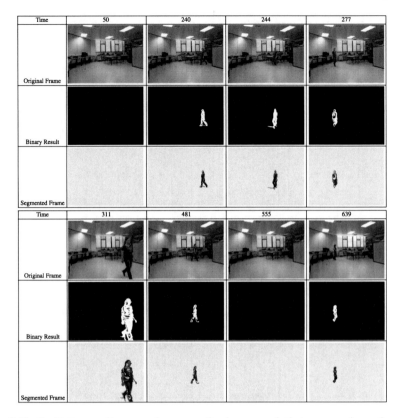

Fig. 2.19 Qualitative results over color perspective images such that a person is continuously entering and leaving our laboratory room. So, the *first row* shows the original frame of the sequence, whereas the last *two rows* illustrate the segmentation result obtained by the **CoD** approach: a binary image representing the background/foreground classification carried out, such that background is represented by *black color* and foreground pixels are coded in *white*; and a color image, where the foreground elements appear as in the original frame, whereas background is coded in an artificial, homogeneous color

At this point, the approach's performance is more accurate by providing less false negatives. Finally, another global illumination change makes the scene very dark. Although the illumination is poor, the proposed approach is capable of detecting the individual. Note that the darker the scene is, the higher the shadow presence is. That is, because the intensity of the shadow pixels is more affected by this phenomenon, their value is different enough from the background pixel brightness to be wrongly labeled as foreground. Moreover, a background element (a chair) is moved. Note that it is not correctly detected both in the new position and the old one. The reason is that when it is moved, it is identified that it is a background element that has started to move. So, the left *hole* is properly covered with the new background. Then, when it is located at the new position, it is adequately identified as a background element, as it can be observed.

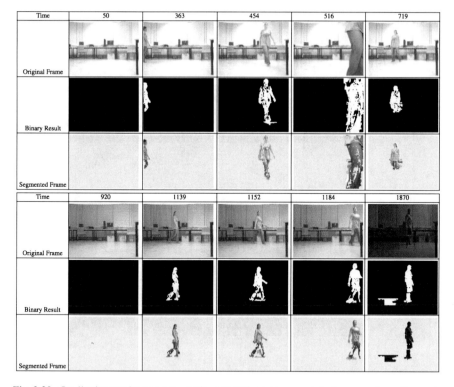

Fig. 2.20 Qualitative results over gray-scale perspective images such that a person is continuously entering and leaving our laboratory room. So, the *first row* shows the original frame of the sequence, whereas the last *two rows* illustrate the segmentation result obtained by the **CoD** approach: a binary image representing the background/foreground classification carried out, such that the background is represented by *black color* and the foreground pixels are coded in *white*; and a color image, where the foreground elements appear as in the original frame, whereas the background is coded in an artificial, homogeneous color

2.3.3.2 Fisheye Image Experiments

In this section, the CoD's performance is assessed over fisheye images. For that, a *DR2-COL-CSBOX* camera with a *Fujinon YV*2.2 × 1.4A-2 1/3" 1.4–3.1 mm CS-Mount lens was used [30, 31]. At this instance, the fisheye camera was located at the center of another laboratory room, pointing upwards, by monitoring the presence of an individual around the visual system. Some examples of the algorithm's performance over this image sequence are depicted in Fig. 2.21, while the set of parameters used is summarized in Table 2.5.

As it can be observed, the performance results are even better than those over perspective images, in spite of the lightning source blink, which is properly corrected by avoiding false positives due to it. Also note that, unlike the perspective images, the proximity to the camera affects in large extent to the pixel intensity values. A

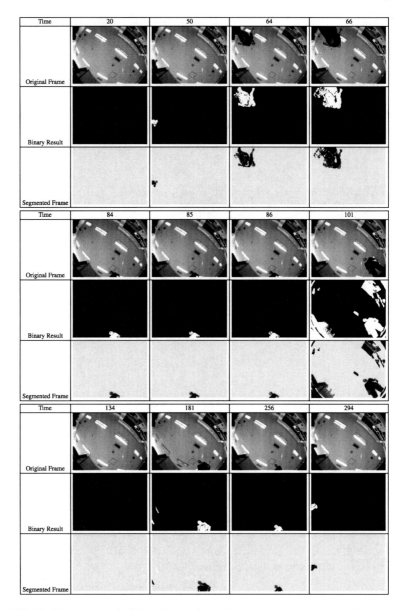

Fig. 2.21 Qualitative results for fisheye images for a video sequence where a person is continuously entering and leaving our laboratory room. So, the *first row* shows the original frame of the sequence, whereas the last *two rows* illustrate the segmentation result obtained by the **CoD** approach: a binary image representing the background/foreground classification carried out, such that the background is represented by *black color* and the foreground pixels are coded in *white*; and a color image, where the foreground elements appear as in the original frame, whereas the background is coded in an artificial, homogeneous color

Table 2.5 Parameter values used for fisheye images when the **CoD** is performed

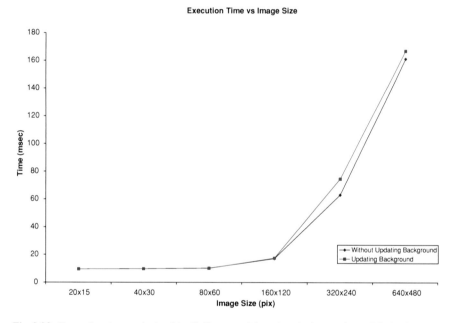

Subimage Size	10° / 15 pix
Erosion Mask	0 1 0 / 0 1 1 / 0 0 0
Dilation Mask	1 1 1 / 1 1 1 / 1 1 1

Fig. 2.22 Execution time analysis of the **CoD** approach based on the image size and the background frame update on an Intel(R) Core(TM) Duo CPU P8700 at 2.53 GHz

sample of this can be observed in frame at time 101 or at time 181. Nevertheless, this temporary change is rightly not considered as a global illumination change. That is why classification in consecutive frames was again successful.

To conclude this section, an execution time analysis is carried out. For that, two different parameters are considered: the image size and the process to update the reference frame for the *background(-frame) subtraction*. The CoD C++ implementation was run on an Intel(R) Core(TM) Duo CPU P8700 at 2.53 GHz by obtaining the execution time depicted in Fig. 2.22. As it can be observed, the execution time is slightly higher when the updating operation is used. However, it is worth noting that it was considered the worst case in which the updating operation was required. In addition, real-time performance is obtained for a 320×240 image resolution.

2.4 Conclusions

In this chapter we have studied the basic case of motion detection, that is, motion detection in scenes with background motionless, aiming at analyzing and solving different issues referred to the use of different imaging sensors, the adaptation to different environments, different motion speed, the shape changes of the targets, or some uncontrolled dynamic factors such as, for instance, gradual/sudden illumination changes. As a solution, a CoD techniques has been proposed. Mainly, it combines a *frame-by-frame difference* together with a *background(-frame) subtraction* with the purpose of overcoming the two well-known difference drawbacks (i.e., *ghosting* and *foreground aperture*). Moreover, on the way to autonomous, robust visual systems, it has also been necessary to study the automatic threshold estimation. For that, a *dynamic* thresholding method based on resolution distribution in an image has been presented. This technique automatically divides the captured images and sets the proper thresholding parameters for two different kinds of cameras: perspective and fisheye. So, problems such as non-uniform-distributed resolution, inadequate illumination gradient in the scene, unsuitable contrast, or the overlapping of the background and the target gray-level distributions, are overcome.

In addition, some experiments over public image datasets and our own image datasets were carried out. Both quantitative and qualitative results have been provided in order to assess the CoD's performance under different conditions. As the experimental results have highlighted, the proposed approach is able to deal with different imaging devices, variable target's speeds or types of interest elements such as people or animals. Furthermore, a comparative analysis with some well-known techniques (those that have provided results on these image datasets) has demonstrated that our approach outperforms them.

Finally, a time-execution analysis has been presented. In that study, two different parameters were considered: the image size and the process to update the reference frame for the *background(-frame) subtraction*. It highlights that the execution time depends on the image size, although a real-time performance is obtained for a 320×240 image resolution. So, the proposed approach can be used for real-time robotic tasks.

References

1. Collins, R., Lipton, A., Kanade, T., Fijiyoshi, H., Duggins, D., Tsin, Y., Tolliver, D., Enomoto, N., Hasegawa, O., Burt, P., Wixson, L.: A system for video surveillance and monitoring. Tech. rep., Carnegie Mellon University, Pittsburg, PA (2000)

2. Kameda, Y., Minoh, M.: A human motion estimation method using 3-successive video frames. In: International Conference on Virtual Systems and Multimedia (VSMM), pp. 135–140. Gifu, Japan (1996)

3. Kanade, T., Collins, R., Lipton, A., Burt, P., Wixson, L.: Advances in cooperative multi-sensor video surveillance. In: Darpa Image Understanding Workshop, vol. I, pp. 3–24. Morgan Kaufmann (1998)

4. Migliore, D., Matteucci, M., Naccari, M.: A revaluation of frame difference in fast and robust motion detection. In: 4th ACM International Workshop on Video Surveillance and Sensor Networks (VSSN), pp. 215–218. Santa Barbara, California (2006)

5. Wren, C., Azarbeyejani, A., Darrell, T., Pentland, A.: Pfinder: Real-time tracking of the human body. IEEE Transactions on Pattern Analysis and Machine Intelligence (PAMI) 19(7), 780–785 (1997)

6. Sezgin, M., Sankur, B.: Survey over image thresholding techniques and quantitative performance evaluation. Journal of Electronic Imaging 13(1), 146–168 (2004)

7. Mičušík, B.: Two view geometry of omnidirectional cameras. Ph.D. thesis, Center for Machine Perception, Czech Technical University in Prague (2004)

8. Toyama, K., Krumm, J., Brumitt, B., Meyers, B.: http://research.microsoft.com/en-us/um/people/jckrumm/WallFlower/TestImages.htm (1999)

9. Hörster, E., Lienhart, R.: http://mmc36.informatik.uni-augsburg.de/VSSN06_OSAC/ (2006)

10. Taj, M.: Surveillance performance evaluation initiative (spevi)—audiovisual people dataset. http://www.elec.qmul.ac.uk/staffinfo/andrea/avss2007_d.html (2007)

11. Ferryman, J.: http://www.cvg.rdg.ac.uk/PETS2006/data.html (2006)

12. Berger, J., Patel, T., Shin, D., Piltz, J., Stone, R.: Computerized stereochronoscopy and alteration flicker to detect optic nerve head contour change. Ophtalmology 107(7) (2000)

13. Hu, J., Kahsi, R., Lopresti, D., Nagy, G., Wilfong, G.: Why table ground-truthing is hard. In: Sixth International Conference on Document Analysis and Recognition, pp. 129–133. Seattle, WA, USA (2001)

14. Rosin, P., Ioannidis, E.: Evaluation of global image thresholding for change detection. Pattern Recognition Letters 24(14), 2345–2356 (2003)

15. Cheung, S., Kamath, C.: Robust techniques for background subtraction in urban traffic video. Electronic Imaging: Video Communications and Image Processing 5308(1), 881–892 (2004)

16. Benezeth, Y., Jodoin, P., Emile, B., Laurent, H., Rosenberger, C.: Review and evaluation of commonly-implemented background subtraction algorithms. In: 19th International Conference on Pattern Recognition (ICPR), pp. 1–4. Tampa, Florida (2008)

17. Davis, J., Goadrich, M.: The relationship between precision-recall and roc curves. In: 23rd International Conference on Machine Learning, pp. 233–240. Pittsburg, Pennsylvania (2006)

18. Stauffer, C., Grimson, W.: Adaptive background mixture models for real-time tracking. In: IEEE Conference on Computer Vision and Pattern Recognition (CVPR), pp. 246–252 (1999)

19. Matsuyama, T., Ohya, T., Habe, H.: Background subtraction for non-stationary scenes. In: Fourth Asian Conference on Computer Vision, pp. 662–667. Singapore (2000)

20. Haritaoglu, I., Harwood, D., Davis, L.: W4: Real-time surveillance of people and their activities. IEEE Transactions on Pattern Analysis and Machine Intelligence (PAMI) 22(8), 809–830 (2000)

21. Nakai, H.: Non-parameterized bayes decision method for moving object detection. In: Asian Conference on Computer Vision. Singapore (1995)

22. Oliver, N., Rosario, B., Pentland, A.: A bayesian computer vision system for modeling human interactions. IEEE Transactions on Pattern Analysis and Machine Intelligence (PAMI) 22(8), 831–843 (2000)

23. Toyama, K., Krum, J., Brumitt, B., Meyers, B.: Wallflower: Principles and practice of background maintenance. In: Seventh IEEE International Conference on Computer Vision (ICCV), vol. 1, pp. 255–261. Kerkyra, Greece (1999)

24. Kottow, D., Koppen, M., del Solar, J.R.: A background maintenance model in the spatial-range domain. In: 2nd ECCV Workshop on Statistical Methods in Video Processing, pp. 141–152. Prague, Czech Republic (2004)

25. Varcheie, P., Sills-Lavoie, M., Bilodeau, G.A.: An efficient region-based background subtraction technique. In: Canadian Conference on Computer and Robot Vision, pp. 71–78 (2008)
26. Cha, S., Srihari, S.: On measuring the distance between histograms. Pattern Recognition **35**(6), 1355–1370 (2002)
27. Max-Planck-Institut-Informatik: http://www.mpi-inf.mpg.de/departments/irg3/software.html (2005)
28. http://www.gifart.de/ (2002)
29. VidereDesign: http://198.144.193.48/index.php?id=31
30. PointGrey: http://www.ptgrey.com/products/dragonfly2/index.asp (2009)
31. Fujinon: http://www.fujinon.com/Security/Product.aspx?cat=1019\&id=74 (2009)

Chapter 3
Motion Detection in General Backgrounds

Abstract Once the basic case of the motion detection problem has been studied and solved the issues referred to the use of different imaging sensors, the adaptation to different environments, different motion speed, the shape changes of the targets, and some uncontrolled dynamic factors (e.g. gradual/sudden illumination changes), we have focused on motion detection when real scenes are considered. Therefore, in this chapter, the goal is to design a *perfect* segmentation technique based on motion in environments without any constraint about the environment and the targets to be identified. With that aim, different issues such as, for instance, the presence of vacillating background elements or the distinction between targets and background objects in terms of motion and motionless situations, have been studied and solved. Thus, a brief review of the previous work is carried out in order to introduce our approach. Then, a deeper analysis of the problems as well as the proposed solutions are explained. Finally, experimental results, from qualitative and quantitative points of view, are presented and discussed. As it will be demonstrated, compared with classical techniques, the proposed algorithm is faster, more robust, and sensor-independent.

Keywords Machine vision · Computer vision · Image segmentation · Background maintenance · Motion detection · Robot vision · Dynamic environments · Visual surveillance

3.1 State of the Art

As previously introduced, motion detection in images of the same scene taken at different times, is of widespread interest due to the large number of applications in diverse disciplines. However, it is a difficult problem to solve when no constraints about targets and environment (especially in terms of the presence of moving background elements) are established. Thus, waving trees, moving water, or blinking screens as part of the background can make the system miserably fail.

E. Martínez-Martín and A. P. del Pobil, *Robust Motion Detection in Real-Life Scenarios*, 43
SpringerBriefs in Computer Science, DOI: 10.1007/978-1-4471-4216-4_3,
© Ester Martínez-Martín 2012

Fig. 3.1 Example of temporal median filtering performance

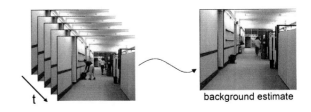

background estimate

Research on this topic has taken a number of forms, although the most extended approach is *background maintenance*. This approach is similar to *background (-frame) subtraction*, but a statistical representation of the scene, which is updated over time, is used as *background model*.

Along this line, one of the first approaches consisted of using a *background (-frame) subtraction* together with a *background update technique* in order to make it more adaptable to the environment [1]. Thus, the background update, for each pixel x, is as follows:

$$B_{t+1}(x) = \alpha F_t(x) + (1 - \alpha) B_t(x) \tag{3.1}$$

where α, called *learning rate*, is kept small to prevent the *ghosting* problem. In that way, there is an appearance compensation of static new objects as well as sudden and fluctuating illumination. Moreover, the used *thresholding method* is followed by a closing operation with a 3×3 kernel for discarding small regions. Note that a *predefined* threshold for the whole image, was employed. However, independently of the pixel classification, the pixel information is considered in the background model computation by polluting it. An improvement to that is to incorporate selective maintenance, which consists of computing the new background model by ignoring the foreground pixels. In a formal way, it can be expressed as:

$$B_{t+1}(x) = \begin{cases} \alpha F_t(x) + (1 - \alpha) B_t(x) & \text{if } F_t(x) \text{ is background} \\ \beta F_t(x) + (1 - \beta) B_t(x) & \text{if } F_t(x) \text{ is foreground} \end{cases} \tag{3.2}$$

Here, the idea is to adapt very quickly a pixel classified as background and very slowly when the pixel is classified as foreground. For this reason, $\beta \ll \alpha$ and usually $\beta = 0$ like in [2]. In spite of providing stability and good accuracy in extracting video objects of relative reduced complexity, it fails when the background is not slow changing and/or targets have any complexity. Besides, the erroneous pixel classification can make permanent a wrong background model.

One way to solve this adaptation problem is to define a statistical model as the average [3] or the median [4–8] of the previous n frames (see Fig. 3.1). Although it is rather a fast approach, it suffers from two important drawbacks. On the one hand, it is very memory-consuming since the memory requirement is $n * size(frame)$. On the other hand, the moving objects that stop for a long time become part of the background and a *ghost* is detected in the area where they were stopped. This will persist for all the following frames which avoid that area from being updated. Despite the improvement introduced by Cucchiara et al. [8] consisting of using knowledge-based background model, it is still a critical issue to be solved. The background model at each pixel location is based on pixel's recent history—just the previous n frames or a weighted average where recent frames have higher weight. In essence, the background model is computed as a chronological average from the pixel history and no spatial correlation is used between different (neighboring) pixel locations.

A relatively recent variant of this method is *Kernel Density Estimators* (KDE) [9]. In this case, the background is provided by the histogram of the n most recent pixel values after being smoothed with a Gaussian kernel (sample-point density estimator). A drawback, apart from the high memory requirement, is the time consumption due to the computation of the kernel values.

Algorithm 1 Joint Difference Algorithm [10]

---

for each pixel x **do**
  if $((|F_t(x) - F_{t-1}(x)| > \tau_t)$ AND $(|F_t(x) - F_{t-2}(x)| > \tau_t))$ **then**
    Foreground Pixel;
  else
    Background Pixel;
  end if
end for
Cluster pixels into connected regions;
for each region R **do**
  for each pixel x **do**
    if $(|F_t(x) - B_t(x)| > \tau_t)$ **then**
      Foreground Pixel;
    end if
  end for
end for
for each pixel x **do**
  if $Foreground\ (x)$ **then**
    $B_{t+1}(x) = B_t(x);$
    $\tau_{t+1}(x) = \tau_t(x)$
  else
    $B_{t+1}(x) = (\alpha * B_t(x)) + ((1 - \alpha) * F_t(x));$
    $\tau_{t+1}(x) = (\alpha * \tau_t(x)) + ((1 - \alpha) * (5 * |F_t(x) - B_t(x)|));$
  end if
end for

As an alternative, Collins et al. [10] proposed a hybrid algorithm that combined an adaptive *background(-frame) subtraction technique* with a *three-frame differencing algorithm* [11]. In fact, as sketched in Algorithm 1, the *three-frame differencing* is used to initially classify pixels as background or foreground. As this method is not generally effective to extract the entire shape of the moving targets, an adaptive *background(-frame) subtraction technique* is applied to recover the entire region. Note that, in Algorithm 1, α represents a time constant that specifies how fast new information supplants old observations, and $\tau_t(x)$ refers to a threshold describing a statistically significant intensity change at pixel position x. In addition, $B_t(x)$ is analogous to a local temporal average of intensity values and $\tau_n(x)$ to 5 times the local temporal standard deviation of intensity, when a non-moving pixel is considered as a temporal series. Both parameters are computed by using an *Infinite Impulse Response* (IIR) filter. Thus, $B_t(x)$ is initially set to the first provided image and $\tau_t(x)$ is initially set to some predetermined, nonzero value.

In spite of seeming that they solve the frame difference drawbacks, the procedure fails when the targets begin or end their motion and/or when there are luminance variations in the scene. Furthermore, it suffers from a few problems on variable depth shots. Another disadvantage is that it is assumed that the background frame is free of foreground objects, since there is no additional processing for the case that assumption is not satisfied.

Wren et al. [12] proposed *Pfinder* where each pixel is fitted to one Gaussian distribution (μ, σ) over the histogram. Thus, the scene background is modeled with a PDF whose update is obtained from a running average as follows:

$$\begin{cases} \mu_{t+1}(x) = \alpha F_t(x) + (1-\alpha)\,\mu_{t-1}(x) \\ \sigma_{t+1}(x) = \alpha\,(F_t(x) - \mu_t(x))^2 + (1-\alpha)\,\sigma_t^2(x) \end{cases} \tag{3.3}$$

where σ_t stands for the covariance matrix over each pixel x at time t. Furthermore, a variable number of dynamic Gaussian distributions are used to obtain models of foreground objects. In that way, they solve the problem of tracking a person in complex scenes in which there is a single unoccluded person and a fixed camera. Nevertheless, it requires an initialization period where the room is empty to provide good results. An extension of that system is *Spfinder* [13] which uses a wide-baseline stereo camera to obtain $3D$ models. In this case, the reported results refer to capture accurate $3D$ movements of head and hands in a smaller desk-area environment. In both systems, it is assumed that there is only a single person and in an upright standing posture. Moreover, there have been no reports on the success of this tracker in outdoor scenes.

With the aim of being able to cope with multiple modal background distributions, Stauffer & Grimson [14] extended the multiple object model to also allow the background model to be a mixture of several Gaussians. Thus, the probability of observing a background pixel x is defined as the following weighted sum:

$$P(x) = \sum_{i=1}^{K} \left[\omega_{i,x,t} * \eta \left(F_{x,t}, \mu_{i,x,t}\sigma_{i,x,t} \right) \right] \tag{3.4}$$

where K is the number of the considered Gaussian distributions; $\omega_{i,x,t}$ is the weight of the ith distribution; $\mu_{i,x,t}$ refers to the mean value of the ith distribution for the pixel x until time t; $\Sigma_{i,x,t}$ represents the corresponding variation matrix that is considered diagonal by computational cost; and $\eta\left(F_{x,t}, \mu_{i,x,t}\sigma_{i,x,t}\right)$ corresponds to the PDF of the ith distribution. Thus, for each frame, every pixel value is checked with the already existing K distributions until a match is found. In this context, a match is defined as follows:

$$|F_{x,t} - \mu_{i,x,t}| \leq (2.5 * \sigma_{i,x,t}) \tag{3.5}$$

Whenever no matches are found, the statistical distribution with the lowest weight is replaced by a new Gaussian with mean $F_{x,t}$, a large initial variance σ_0 and a small weight ω_0. Moreover, the remaining parameters of a matched component (i.e. the Gaussian model for which $F_{x,t}$ is within 2.5 standard deviations of its mean) are updated as follows:

$$\begin{cases} \omega_{i,x,t} = (1 - \alpha)\,\omega_{i,x,t-1} + \alpha \\ \mu_{i,x,t} = (1 - \rho)\,\mu_{i,x,t-1} + \rho\,F_{i,x,t} \\ \sigma_{i,x,t}^2 = (1 - \rho)\,\sigma_{i,x,t-1}^2 + \rho\left(F_{i,x,t} - \mu_{i,x,t}\right)^2 \end{cases} \tag{3.6}$$

such that α is a user-defined learning rate and ρ is a second learning rate defined as $\rho = \alpha\eta\left(F_{i,x,t}, \mu_{i,x,t}, \Sigma_{i,x,t}\right)$. The μ and σ parameters of unmatched distributions remain the same, while their weight is reduced as follows: $\omega_{i,x,t} = (1 - \alpha)\,\omega_{i,x,t-1}$ to achieve decay.

Once every Gaussian has been updated, the K weights $\omega_{i,x,t}$ are normalized so that they sum up to 1. Then, the K distributions are ordered based on a fitness value $\omega_{i,x,t}/\sigma_{i,x,t}$ and then only the H most reliable distributions are chosen as part of the background:

$$H = \text{argmin}_h\left(\sum_{i=1}^{h} \omega_i > \tau\right) \tag{3.7}$$

where τ is a threshold. Then, those pixels which are at more 2.5 standard deviations away from any of those H distributions are labeled *in motion*, that is, as foreground.

Nevertheless, note that the *Mixture of Gaussians* (MoG) actually models both the foreground and the background which implies that a foreground object that stops for a period of time is identified as background. On the contrary, if a stopped object, modeled as background, starts moving, a *hole* is left behind them by generating false alarms until the new Gaussian distribution has a weight high enough to carry out a right classification. Another drawback is the way the Gaussian distributions are initialized. This process, called *training period*, consists of observing an empty scene for several seconds by considering background everything seen. However, in real environments, it is not possible to guarantee that no foreground elements enter the scene during that *training period*. Another issue is how to update the statistical distributions over time such that the H considered distributions for background classification correctly refer to background values. Moreover, the number of Gaussian distributions is arbitrarily predefined by the user (usually between 3 and 5), although a greater number could be required in some situations.

In addition, from a comparative point of view, although Gao et al. [15] determined that the MoG approach is indeed a better representation of backgrounds even in static scenes from comparing the assumption of a single versus MoG to model the background, a recent comparative study [16] of five common algorithms based on 29 video sequences with three categories, including multi-modal and noisy ones, concluded that a basic background subtraction algorithm with simple updating outperformed KDE and temporal derivative and was equivalent to a single Gaussian or MoG for videos in the first noise-free uni-modal category. In addition, results for a single Gaussian were surprisingly good for multi-modal videos, and comparable to MoG. Finally, the single Gaussian, KDE and MoG resulted in good and equivalent results for noisy videos.

3.2 Mixture of Differences (MoD) Approach

As mentioned above, statistical distributions are used to work on multi-modal environments. However, there are still some issues to be overcome. Keeping in mind the goal to obtain an *ideal* method for motion detection, the issues to be solved can be classified into four different categories:

1. the management of a training period with foreground objects in dynamic, real environments
2. the adaptation to minor dynamic, uncontrolled changes such as the passage of time, blinking of screen, or shadows
3. the adaptation to sudden, unexpected changes in illumination
4. the distinction between foreground and background objects in terms of motion and motionless situations.

We propose a hybrid technique composed of a *background maintenance* process with a *frame-difference combination* technique. Therefore, two different stages take place:

1. *Training period*: a scene is observed during several seconds in order to build a starting statistical background model without any assumption about the presence/absence of foreground elements during this period
2. *Segmentation period*: once an initial background model is built, both an image segmentation and a background model updating phase start.

3.2.1 Training Period

This first phase consists of building an initial statistical background model. With the aim to work on real, dynamic environments, the first issue to be solved is dealing with the presence of foreground objects during the whole stage. For that, the method presented in the previous chapter is used, that is, **CoD**, which combines a *temporal adjacent frame differencing* with *a subtraction(-frame) technique* by setting as reference frame the first image taken. As previously pointed out, the proper combination of both methods allows successfully solving the difference drawbacks.

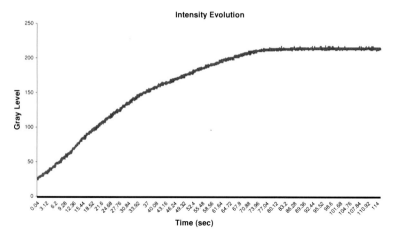

Fig. 3.2 Pixel value evolution along time at pixel $(157, 6)$ on *Time of Day* video sequence from *Wallflower* dataset [17]

Moreover, thanks to the incorporation of a target detection technique when targets stop or start moving in the scene, a good performance is provided in different kinds of environments.

Nevertheless, a drawback of the **CoD** technique is that it can have problems with vacillating background elements, such as the blinking of screens or the swaying of trees. As a consequence, it has been necessary to design a way to detect and solve that situation. In our case, a size criterion to distinguish the objects of interest from the moving background elements, has been established. Of course, the size threshold value depends on the position of the camera with respect to the observed scene as well as the image size, since these two factors determine the size of the targets in terms of pixels. Experimentally, this parameter value was set to 30 pixels for an image resolution of 160×120, 384×240, 388×288 and 640×480 pixels and for both perspective and fisheye images, by obtaining a good performance in all the cases, as it will be presented in the following sections.

Another important issue in this stage is the changes in illumination. The first case under study is the global unexpected changes in illumination. As previously, the target's proximity to the camera is considered to trigger an alarm of this kind. Hence, it is assumed a global illumination has occurred when more than two-thirds of the image is classified as foreground and the amount of foreground pixels in the current frame is greater than 1.5 times the amount in the previous frame. Note that it is assumed that if a global illumination change occurs, a disruptive event takes place and, therefore, the whole process needs to be restarted; that is, the statistical model built until now is reset and this stage starts again. Take into account that, as introduced in the previous section, some lighting sources need several milliseconds to stabilize. Therefore, with the aim of having reliable information as starting knowledge, the system waits for some frames (typically 5) before reinitialization.

Second, the gradual illumination changes were considered. Note that the pixel values change along time even though nothing is changing (see Fig. 3.2). Thus, given that there is no update process in the **CoD** technique, except for the case in which a background element starts moving, it was analyzed how long this stage should take to obtain a reliable initial background model without integrating a background update method. As shown in Fig. 3.2, the background information is not suitable to properly segment images from second 5. Therefore, it was experimentally stated that this stage should take, as maximum, 100 frames, i.e., 4 s at a video rate of 25 fps.

Once a binary image resulting from the previous segmentation process is obtained, the background pixel information is incorporated into the statistical scene model to be built, namely a single-Gaussian model. Note that this is made after two consecutive morphological operations (erosion followed by dilation) are applied to erase isolated pixels as a result of segmentation errors due to dynamic factors such as sensor noise, non-uniform attenuation, or lighting blinking.

3.2.2 Segmentation Period

The second phase carries out motion detection and properly updates the background model built in the previous stage. For that, a mixture of three difference approaches is used: *temporal adjacent frame difference*, *background(-frame) subtraction* and *background maintenance*.

The first two methods are combined as in the **CoD** technique, but in this case, the reference frame used for *background(-frame) subtraction* is set to the mean of the Gaussian distribution modeling the background obtained in the preceding phase. Although it can be thought that it would be enough to only use *background(-frame) subtraction* to obtain a raw classification, it is a wrong hypothesis since it can be possible that some pixels lack enough information to model them with a reliable Gaussian distribution. The reason can be segmentation errors or the continuous presence of foreground objects at those image positions during the *training period*.

Thus, once a raw classification of scene pixels is obtained from the **CoD** technique, the statistical background model is used to refine it. The designed background maintenance technique classifies the pixels as follows:

$$\begin{cases} |F_t(x) - \mu_t(x)| > (k_x * \sigma_t(x)) & \text{foreground} \\ \text{otherwise} & \text{background} \end{cases} \qquad (3.8)$$

where $\mu_t(x)$ and $\sigma_t(x)$ correspond, respectively, to the mean and the standard deviation defining the Gaussian distribution for each pixel x at time t; and k_x $(0.0 < k_x \leq 3.0)$ is a factor established for each pixel, since the pixel fluctuation depends on the pixel position within the scene, being higher at the borders, where errors are more common than at the center of the image. This factor is computed from the values making up the model for that pixel at each moment. It is worth noting that, in the case that no information is available for any pixel, this factor is initially set to a predetermined, nonzero value in order to obtain a proper segmentation until statistical information for that pixel is provided. A similar problem arises with σ, since it could never converge to the right value if it is initially set to zero when there is a lack of information.

Therefore, a pixel is classified as foreground when both the **CoD** technique and the *background maintenance method* labeled it as foreground, or when there is no statistical information about the pixel and the **CoD** technique categorized it as foreground.

After segmenting an image, two consecutive morphological operations are applied to erase isolated points or lines caused by small dynamic factors. Then, while the foreground pixels can be processed by applying a tracking method or a recognition module depending on the particular task to be achieved, the pixels classified as background are incorporated into the adaptive background model. For that, the following equations are used:

$$\begin{cases} \mu_t(x) = \begin{cases} (1-\alpha)\,\mu_{t-1}(x) + \alpha F_t(x) & \text{if background} \\ \mu_{t-1}(x) & \text{otherwise} \end{cases} \\ \sigma_t(x) = \begin{cases} (1-\alpha)\,\sigma_t(x) + (\alpha\,(F_t(x) - \mu_t)^2 & \text{if background} \\ \sigma_t(x) & \text{otherwise} \end{cases} \end{cases} \tag{3.9}$$

Here, the constant α ($0 < \alpha < 1$) is the learning rate used in the Gaussian model. It is obtained from the number of samples for the model as $\alpha = 1.0/N$. Note that α value controls the speed at which the model adapts to changes. Its small value when a lot of samples are considered, makes the Gaussian distribution adapt too slowly to background changes as shown in Fig. 3.3a. Therefore, after a certain period of time, the background model cannot be suitable for the foreground pixel detection. For that reason, a mechanism for its effective maintenance was designed. Thus, at each iteration:

• the background model is being updated with each new frame using Eq. 3.9
• a new background model is being built in parallel using the recent history of the segmentation results.

In this way, the background model as well as the reference frame for the *background(-frame) subtraction*, are replaced, after some time, by a more suitable, new one. In our experiments, this update takes place after 200 frames and, as depicted in Fig. 3.3b, the error has been considerably reduced and the model is more robustly adapted to those quick changes.

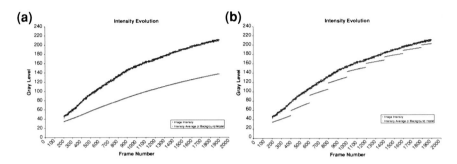

Fig. 3.3 History of Gaussian mean of the background model versus pixel gray level evolution along time at pixel (157, 6) on *Time of Day* video sequence from Wallflower dataset [17]. **a** Gaussian mean evolution versus scene gray level evolution when model is updated by using Eq. 3.9. **b** Gaussian mean evolution versus scene gray level evolution when model is continuously updated

Table 3.1 Parameters used for evaluating the **MoD**'s performance over the three considered image datasets (*Wallflower Dataset* [17], *VSSN06* [18] and *Audiovisual People Dataset* [19])

Subimage Size	10x10		
Nframes for Initial Background Model	200		
Erosion Mask	0	1	0
	0	1	1
	0	0	0
Dilation Mask	1	1	1
	1	1	1
	1	1	1

3.3 Experimental Results

As in the previous chapter, two different kinds of experiments are presented. On the one hand, a qualitative and quantitative performance analysis is done over three image datasets of the literature: *Wallflower Dataset* [17], *VSSN06* [18] and *Audiovisual People Dataset* [19]. On the other hand, qualitative results over our own dataset composed of both perspective and fisheye images are presented.

3.3.1 Experimental Results Over Image Datasets

For each background subtraction technique, there are some sets of parameters that should be determined. The set of parameters used by our technique for the considered image datasets is listed in Table 3.1. Note that these parameters were not changed during the whole datasets.

Fig. 3.4 Mean intensity of the initial background model built for the seven canonical background problems contained in *Wallflower* dataset [17]

3.3.1.1 Wallflower Dataset

In this case, as the goal is to evaluate the **MoD**'s performance without any constraint, the seven video sequences that compose this image dataset, are considered. Again, the obtained experimental results are compared with other well-known techniques that have provided results for this dataset such as MoG, Eigenbackground, or temporal derivative.

Thus, with the purpose of carrying out a proper comparison, the number of frames to build the initial background model (i.e. frames used for the training period) was 200, as pointed out in the dataset. Figure 3.4 presents the initial background model obtained for each video sequence under study, while Fig. 3.5 presents a qualitative comparison between the result of the **MoD** algorithm, the one obtained by other well-known approaches and the provided hand-segmented version. In addition, a quantitative evaluation is presented in terms of True Positive Rate (TPR) (Fig. 3.6), False Positive Rate (FPR) (Fig. 3.7), of *recall* and *precision* measurements (Table 3.2) and of other statistical measurements (Table 3.3).

Thus, in the first image sequence, *Moved Object*, a conference room is observed. The background is initially still (during approximately 240 frames) until a person enters the scene, sits on a chair, and makes a call. Then, the person leaves the scene, but both the chair and the telephone have been moved as a consequence of his actions. The goal is to properly classify those two elements as background and not as foreground. As shown qualitatively in Fig. 3.5 and quantitatively in Table 3.2, the background elements were correctly classified. This is because of the incorporation into the algorithm of the distinction between an element momentarily stopped from that which has started moving. Thus, when they are initially moved, the algorithm detects that they are background elements that have changed their location in the scene. For that reason, the initial position is considered new background and its information is incorporated into the background model. Although those elements should be classified as foreground by the algorithm definition, since the case of a background element starting moving is not explicitly different from the situation where a background element is moved to take a new location, this is not the case. The reason is that the two situations are implicitly considered in the algorithm. In the case of a background element that has been moved to take a different location in the scene, another element has to do the action, i.e., a foreground element takes the background object and puts it in a different place. This fact makes the background element be momentarily part of another foreground element. Therefore, when the

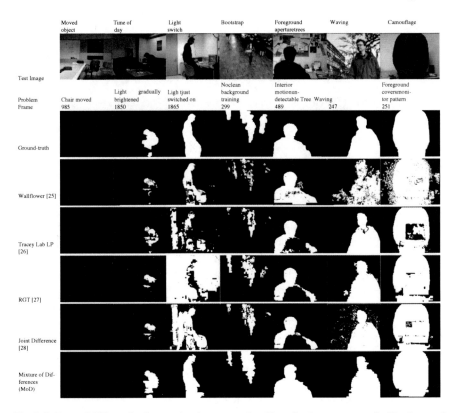

Fig. 3.5 Tests of different background maintenance algorithms for the seven canonical background problems contained in *Wallflower* dataset [17]. Each *row* shows the results of one algorithm, and each *column* represents one image sequence. The *top row* shows the image in the sequence at which the processing was stopped. The *second row* shows hand-segmented images of the foreground used as *ground-truth* for a quantitative comparison

background element is left, the algorithm does not consider it as a new foreground element, by classifying that element as a background unless it keeps moving.

Second, the *Time-of-day* sequence presents a laboratory where a gradual light change takes place. The initial dark scene becomes brighter and a person enters the scene, sits on a sofa, and starts to read a book. In this case, the ability of adapting to gradual changes in illumination is evaluated. Again, as it can be observed in Fig. 3.5 and in Table 3.2, the results are successful thanks to the process to update the background model that allows it to easily adapt to these kinds of changes.

Another event that can modify the pixel values, is a sudden illumination change. This fact is studied with the *Light-switch* image sequence, where a person enters a scene with lights off, turns on the lights, closes the door, and sits at a computer. Note that, apart from the illumination event, the algorithm must properly detect that a background element, the door, has changed its location (both when the person enters

Table 3.2 Comparison of the experimental quantitative results, in terms of *recall* and *precision*, obtained for different segmentation methods on all the *Wallflower* benchmarks [17]

Algorithm	Measurement	Time of day	Light switch	Bootstrap	Foreground aperture	Waving trees	Camoubflage	Total
Mixture of Gaussians [20]	Recall	34.88	49.82	35.93	51.37	77.50	96.23	70.28
	Precision	96.43	10.27	82.89	82.96	93.04	76.65	52.75
Block correlation [21]	Recall	33.46	72.86	9.81	76.66	43.50	42.23	48.11
	Precision	79.33	44.82	89.13	75.79	85.10	88.73	68.25
Temporal derivative [22]	Recall	25.65	76.89	16.99	59.20	57.78	81.40	62.91
	Precision	20.26	17.44	13.21	93.20	18.14	97.08	34.20
Bayesian decision [23]	Recall	34.24	26.86	26.74	50.00	89.30	85.44	65.00
	Precision	48.53	6.11	22.05	55.97	94.02	80.91	47.23
Eigenbackground [24]	Recall	43.22	70.44	89.61	51.39	82.54	96.69	79.58
	Precision	97.66	86.36	29.95	82.78	70.24	86.84	66.48
Wallflower [25]	Recall	37.92	51.29	30.77	93.63	84.17	89.41	76.23
	Precision	95.92	81.65	71.15	87.87	71.23	77.73	78.43
Tracey LAB LP [26]	Recall	50.13	39.61	32.51	52.15	96.75	81.09	68.14
	Precision	93.49	38.91	91.18	88.03	97.67	99.20	87.92
RGT [27]	Recall	29.09	51.19	57.76	50.18	99.51	94.61	76.24
Joint difference [28]	Recall	44.90	85.68	60.34	51.20	99.07	94.04	80.77
	Precision	99.00	44.04	91.40	83.34	86.68	98.66	81.76
Mixture of differences (MoD)	Recall	87.92	93.15	65.50	95.18	98.32	95.63	**92.39**
	Precision	81.50	94.05	82.06	93.85	94.32	99.19	**94.05**

the scene and when he closes it) without being classified as foreground as in *Tracey Lab LP* or *Joint Difference* algorithms (see Fig. 3.5). From the parameter values, the global illumination change is detected when the person switches on the lights at frame 1852. Then, the proposed approach waits for a few frames with the aim of guaranteeing the stability in the illumination sources whichever they are and restarts the segmentation process again by resetting the background model and beginning to gather information to build a new initial background model. Therefore, in this case, the result is only generated by the combination of the *background(-frame) subtraction* with the *temporal adjacent frame differencing* (i.e. the **CoD** algorithm). With regard to the *door* issue, after the reinitiation of the segmentation process, the only part which is detected, is its border. That is classified as background when it is completely closed, since the foreground part is already not visible. Take into account that the only information that is being used is that related to the pixel values. As a consequence, it is not possible to identify the door as previously observed. However, that information could be introduced into the system to increase its robustness in view of these kinds of situations.

Regarding the *Bootstrap* image sequence, a training period without foreground elements is not available. Basically, a cafeteria condiment bar is observed during several minutes. As depicted in Fig. 3.4, the initial background model has been built free of foreground elements, except for a person on the upper right side of the image. It is because that person stopped in that place and, despite controlling this kind of situations, the person was classified as background after being occluded by other foreground elements because no tracking process is applied at this point and he is not moving after that. Something similar has happened with the other semi-transparent ghosts appearing in front of the condiment bar, which makes the segmentation process hard in that area. The no-detection in the test image of the person in front of the condiment bar highlights this fact, although that is not the case for the other target people appearing in the test image whose detection has been quite accurate.

The next considered problem (*Foreground-aperture*) is a person who is sleeping on his desk and starts moving when he wakes up. Here, the difficulty lies on the fact that the sleeping person is initially modeled as part of the background. In addition, the test image is a few frames after the target person starts moving. This makes the model adaptation process more difficult. However, the segmentation goal is achieved thanks to the feedback information provided to the algorithm in each iteration, since it allows to adapt the model in the proper way to detect the awake person almost completely, as shown in Fig. 3.4.

In the end, the vacillating background influence is assessed in two different image sequences. In the first case, the *Waving-trees* image sequence is where an outdoor scene is analyzed. A person appears in a scene which is mainly composed of a swaying tree. The oscillation of the tree prevents to obtain accurate information when the initial background model is being built. Actually, as depicted in Fig. 3.4, the tree branches are modeled in a blurred way. As a consequence, the target silhouette generated for the test image is slightly rough instead of smooth.

On the other hand, the *Camouflage* image sequence is analyzed. In this case, an indoor scene where there is a blinking screen of a computer, is observed. After several frames (240 approximately), a person enters the scene and locates in front of the monitor. Unlike the previous study case, the initial background model contains the information on the screen (see Fig. 3.4). Take into account that the similarity of the pixel values of the target element and the blinking screen as well as the proximity of the camera to the oscillating element, produce an increase in the number of *false negatives* (e.g. see the experimental results provided by the *Tracey Lab LP* or *Joint Difference* algorithms in Fig. 3.4). These problems are overcome by the proposed algorithm by means of the feedback information provided in each frame together with the detection of stop-moving.

From a quantitative point of view, it can be claimed that the **MoD** outperforms the previous approaches' performance, although the proposed approach does not have the better results for both *recall* and *precision* measurements in all the video sequences. Thus, despite the fact that another algorithm can achieve a better result for a measurement in any situation, it is at the cost of obtaining a bad result for the other measurement. That is, there is no video sequence for which a previous algorithm overcomes the performance of the **MoD** in both *recall* and *precision*, as shown in Table 3.2.

Furthermore, a quantitative comparison in terms of TPR and FPR is presented. Thus, as TPR evaluates the foreground pixel classification, a high TPR means that the number of foreground pixels correctly classified is much larger than the number of foreground pixels misclassified as background. Focusing on the results presented in Fig. 3.6, the TPR value is greater than the one obtained by the previous approaches, except for the *Waving-trees* and *Camouflage* image sequences where the difference with the best result is less than 0.01. Also note that the lowest TPR value corresponds to the *Bootstrap* sequence since one of its targets was wrongly missed.

As mentioned above, an evaluation only based on the TPR measurement is not enough to be able to conclude anything about an algorithm's performance since it is just about the actual foreground pixels. Thus, it is also necessary to investigate the influence of the real background pixels in the extracted foreground. For that, the FPR is used given that it measures how many background pixels are correctly classified as background. Note that the best technique should have the highest TPR value, but the lowest FPR value because a high FPR value means that most parts of the image are detected as foreground making the background subtraction technique under study not appropriate to achieve our final goal. As it can be observed in Fig. 3.7, the FPR is low. Actually, the proposed approach combines the highest TPR value and the lowest FPR value in the total evaluation as well as in most of the video sequences. Therefore, our segmentation process outperforms the previous algorithm results. Note that no results for the *Moved Object* video sequence are provided. It is due to TPR and FPR values of all background subtraction techniques that are equal or close to zero.

Moreover, with the aim of carrying out a deeper quantitative analysis, Table 3.3 provides a larger list of statistical measurements that allow us to validate the proposed approach in a more accurate way. First, TNR which expresses how many positives are wrongly tagged, is presented. Again, a high value means a more accurate

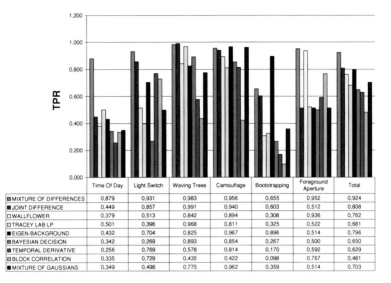

	Time Of Day	Light Switch	Waving Trees	Camouflage	Bootstrapping	Foreground Aperture	Total
MIXTURE OF DIFFERENCES	0,879	0,931	0,983	0,956	0,655	0,952	0,924
JOINT DIFFERENCE	0,449	0,857	0,991	0,940	0,603	0,512	0,808
WALLFLOWER	0,379	0,513	0,842	0,894	0,308	0,936	0,762
TRACEY LAB LP	0,501	0,396	0,968	0,811	0,325	0,522	0,681
EIGEN-BACKGROUND	0,432	0,704	0,825	0,967	0,896	0,514	0,796
BAYESIAN DECISION	0,342	0,269	0,893	0,854	0,267	0,500	0,650
TEMPORAL DERIVATIVE	0,256	0,769	0,578	0,814	0,170	0,592	0,629
BLOCK CORRELATION	0,335	0,729	0,435	0,422	0,098	0,767	0,481
MIXTURE OF GAUSSIANS	0,349	0,498	0,775	0,962	0,359	0,514	0,703

Fig. 3.6 True positive rate (TPR) of different background subtraction techniques for all the video sequences of the *Wallflower* dataset [17], by including an extra *column*, *Total*, that represents the result obtained for all the videos combined together. Note that, as TPR evaluates the foreground pixel classification, a high TPR value means that the number of foreground pixels correctly classified is much larger than the number of foreground pixels misclassified as background

segmentation. The high value obtained for all the video sequences means that a few background pixels were wrongly tagged as foreground. As in the case of FPR, TNR cannot be the only criterion for the evaluation of a background subtraction technique. As a complementary measurement, NPV is used. Hence, how many foreground pixels have been wrongly classified as background is now evaluated. Again, a high value of this parameter refers to a more accurate performance.

On the contrary, TNR measurement can be complemented with FDR whether we are more interested in evaluating the error rate with respect to misclassified background pixels, namely, the percentage of background pixels erroneously tagged as foreground. From that definition, a good performance will provide a low value for this parameter. As it can be checked in Table 3.3, the obtained percentage is lower than 10 %, except for the *Time-of-day* and *Bootstrap* video sequences which show a higher value for this measurement (lower than 20 %).

The following measurements provide a global evaluation for the algorithm's performance since they take into account both the pixels correctly classified and the wrongly ones. The first considered one is *accuracy*. Mathematically speaking, *accuracy* will be higher when lower classification errors are made. Thus, an *accuracy* of 100 % is desired. As shown in Table 3.3, the obtained value for this measurement is around 97 % in almost all the video sequences. In fact, only the *Bootstrap* video sequence provides a lower value. A target person who was missed, has produced a higher level of *FN* and, therefore, a lower value for the *accuracy*.

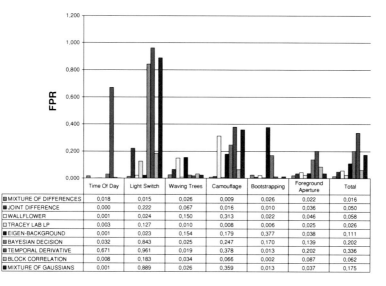

	Time Of Day	Light Switch	Waving Trees	Camouflage	Bootstrapping	Foreground Aperture	Total
▣ MIXTURE OF DIFFERENCES	0,018	0,015	0,026	0,009	0,026	0,022	0,016
▪ JOINT DIFFERENCE	0,000	0,222	0,067	0,016	0,010	0,036	0,050
▢ WALLFLOWER	0,001	0,024	0,150	0,313	0,022	0,046	0,058
▢ TRACEY LAB LP	0,003	0,127	0,010	0,008	0,006	0,025	0,026
▪ EIGEN-BACKGROUND	0,001	0,023	0,154	0,179	0,377	0,038	0,111
▣ BAYESIAN DECISION	0,032	0,843	0,025	0,247	0,170	0,139	0,202
▪ TEMPORAL DERIVATIVE	0,671	0,961	0,019	0,378	0,013	0,202	0,336
▣ BLOCK CORRELATION	0,008	0,183	0,034	0,066	0,002	0,087	0,062
▪ MIXTURE OF GAUSSIANS	0,001	0,889	0,026	0,359	0,013	0,037	0,175

Fig. 3.7 False positive rate (FPR) of different background subtraction techniques for all the video sequences of the *Wallflower* dataset [17], by including an additional column, *Total*, which contains the FPR for all the videos combined together. FPR is used to measure how many background pixels are correctly classified as background. Therefore, the best segmentation technique will have the lowest FPR value

Table 3.3 Quantitative results obtained for the **MoD** approach over the *Wallflower* dataset [17] such that the first three measurements (TNR, NPV, and FDR) provide a performance's evaluation related to misclassified/correctly classified pixels, whereas the rest of the measurements provide a global assessment of the algorithm's performance

	Time of day	Light switch	Boots trap	Foreground aperture	Waving trees	Camouflage	Total
TNR	98.25	98.53	97.43	97.79	97.39	99.05	98.38
NPV	98.93	98.60	94.02	98.28	99.24	94.88	97.90
FDR	18.50	7.20	17.94	6.15	5.68	0.81	5.95
Accuracy	97.42	97.61	92.56	97.11	97.67	97.17	97.01
MCC	0.83	0.92	0.69	0.93	0.95	0.94	0.91
F_1 Score	0.85	0.93	0.73	0.95	0.96	0.97	0.93
JC	0.73	0.87	0.57	0.90	0.93	0.95	0.87
YC	0.80	0.91	0.76	0.92	0.94	0.94	0.92

Thus, high values for TNR, NPV, accuracy, MCC, F_1 score, JC and YC, and low values of FDR result in an accurate segmentation

Another way to validate the system is based on the *MCC* value. In essence, it is a balance measurement that provides information about the correlation between pixels correctly tagged and those wrongly classified. Thus, values near 1, as the ones obtained for the proposed approach, mean an accurate segmentation.

Something similar happens with F_1 *Score*, which is a kind of average of *precision* and *recall* measurements. It reaches its best value at 1. Most of the studied video sequences present a value very close to 1. Again, the *Time-of-day* and *Bootstrap* video sequences achieve the lowest values for this measurement since they present a lower *precision* and/or *recall* values.

With regard to the *JC* measurement, it evaluates the algorithm's accuracy when the foreground pixels are considered. Thus, a low error rate will provide *JC* values around 1. Although the *Bootstrap* video sequence presents a lower value, the rest of the video sequences have achieved values close to 1, by highlighting the efficiency of our algorithm over different conditions.

Finally, the *YC* value expresses the relationship between foreground and background pixels correctly tagged and its value oscillates between 1 and -1, by providing a better performance when it is around 1. As illustrated in Table 3.3, the high obtained values make our approach appropriate for the task which it was designed for.

3.3.1.2 VSSN06

Regarding the *VSSN06* dataset [18], the performance was evaluated over its 8 of 12 video sequences. Thus, in its *video sequence 1*, an indoor scene without oscillating elements, is the background where a virtual girl is moving around. In this case, the *training period* is free of foreground objects. Therefore, the number of frames required to build the initial background model can be reduced. However, for comparative reasons, the value of this parameter is kept during all the experiments over this computer vision dataset. As it can be observed in Fig. 3.8, the target girl has been successfully detected in all frames, even when it partially appears in the scene (e.g. frame 105). No ground-truth information has been provided for this video sequence. That is why only qualitative results are presented.

Moreover, **MoD**'s performance has been checked when a more reduced number of frames (i.e. 15 frames) are used to build the statistical background model (see Fig. 3.9 (for comparative reasons the same sample frames of Fig. 3.8 are shown)). Again, an accurate performance has been obtained.

In a similar way, *video sequence 2* represents an indoor scene where no oscillating elements appear. In this case, the target elements are two boys who are dancing along the whole scene. Again, it is possible to define a *training period* without foreground elements. Some of the obtained results for this video sequence are depicted in Fig. 3.10. As it can be seen, the detection was successful in all the cases, independently of the fact that there are one or two target elements in the scene. In quantitative terms, Table 3.4 highlights the good performance of the proposed approach with a low value of FPR and FDR, while the rest of the measurements have a high value. As a consequence, it can be said that the algorithm also provides a good performance for this video sequence.

Again, an experiment where less frames were used to build the initial statistical background model, has been carried out (see Fig. 3.11). The criteria to state the good performance of a segmentation method are also satisfied (see Table 3.4).

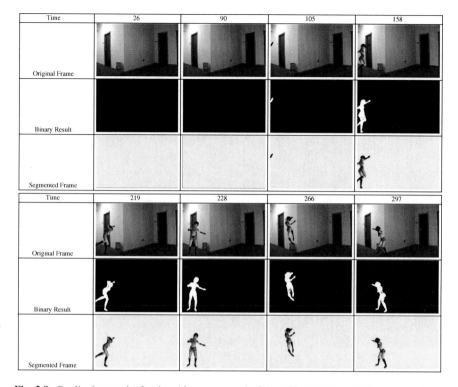

Fig. 3.8 Qualitative results for the *video sequence 1* of the *VSSN06* dataset [18], where a virtual girl is moving around an indoor scene without oscillating elements. Thus, the *first row* of each block shows the original frame of the sequence, while the *other rows* depict the segmentation result obtained by the **MoD** approach: a binary image representing the background/foreground classification carried out, such that the background is represented by *black* and the foreground pixels are coded in *white*; and an image, where the foreground elements appear as in the original frame, whereas the background is coded in an *artificial, homogeneous color*

Vacillating background is considered in the *video sequence 3* and the *video sequence 4*. Both of them show an outdoor scene composed of a garden whose elements oscillate along time. Actually, the difference between them lies on the foreground element to be detected. It is a boy in the first sequence, while it is a girl in the second case.

Thus, both video sequences start with a *training period* without foreground elements. After that, the target element enters the scene and moves around it. Note that the tight similarity between the element of interest and the background intensities have made segmentation task harder in the *video sequence 3*, although it was possible to detect the virtual boy in practically all the frames (see Fig. 3.12).

On the contrary, the results obtained for the *video sequence 4* were more successful as shown in Fig. 3.13. As previously pointed out, the main reason is that the pixel intensities of the target element are more different from the background

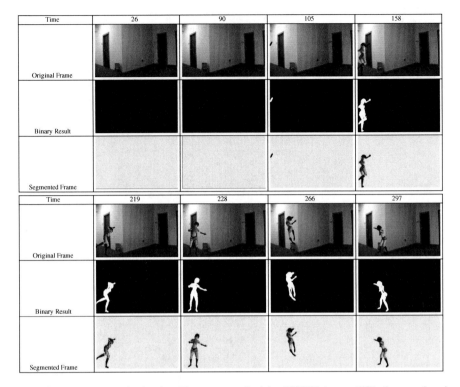

Fig. 3.9 Qualitative results for the *video sequence 1* of the *VSSN06* dataset [18] when a reduced number of frames for building the initial statistical background model has been used. Thus, the *first row* of each block shows the original frame of the sequence, while the *other rows* depict the segmentation result obtained by the **MoD** approach: a binary image representing the background/foreground classification carried out, such that the background is represented by *black color* and the foreground pixels are coded in *white*; and a color image, where the foreground elements appear as in the original frame, whereas the background is coded in an *artificial, homogeneous color*

ones. However, the quantitative results for these two video sequences, summarized in Table 3.4, are not so satisfactory as in the previous cases. It is because some *false positives* occur until the algorithm was capable of properly distinguishing between oscillating pixels belonging to the background and those which compose the target.

Regarding the *video sequence 5*, as in the *video sequences 1* and *2*, a static indoor scene is used as background. The particularity of this sequence is the lack of a *training period* without foreground elements. In addition, two different kinds of target elements are considered. On the one hand, a virtual human being who is dancing around the scene; and, on the other hand, a cat which is walking around the scene. Thus this video sequence assesses both the presence of foreground elements during the *training period* and the detection of target elements different from human beings. As mentioned above, the *training period* covers the first 200 frames. At the beginning of that period, the foreground element, the human being, has slightly

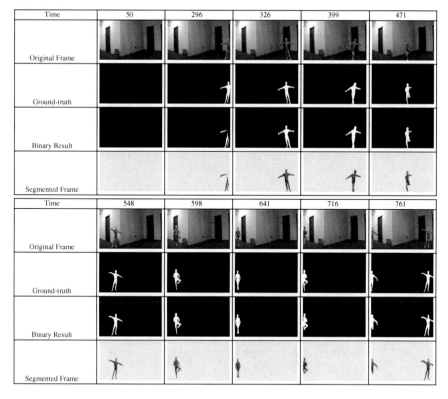

Fig. 3.10 Qualitative results for the *video sequence 2* of the *VSSN06* dataset [18], where two virtual boys are dancing along an indoor scene where no oscillating elements appear. Thus, the *first row* shows the original frame of the sequence, the *second row* depicts the ground-truth frame, and the *last two rows* illustrate the segmentation result obtained by the **MoD** approach: a binary image representing the background/foreground classification carried out, such that the background is represented by *black color* and the foreground pixels are coded in *white*; and a color image, where the foreground elements appear as in the original frame, whereas the background is coded in an *artificial, homogeneous color*

moved from its initial position. For that reason, the algorithm cannot distinguish between the case it is a background element which has moved or, on the contrary, it is a foreground element that has entered the scene. Consequently, the *ghosting* problem cannot be suppressed as it can be observed in the first frame depicted in Fig. 3.15. Nevertheless, when the foreground element leaves its initial position in the background, the proposed approach detects that a foreground element, initially classified as background, starts moving. Therefore, the left *hole* is properly updated with the new background information. As a result, that foreground element is not part of the initial statistical background model (see Fig. 3.14). After solving the *ghosting* problem, the **MoD** algorithm provides a successful segmentation of both the virtual man and the cat. From a quantitative point of view, it is kept as the relationship

Table 3.4 Quantitative results obtained for the **MoD** approach over the *VSSN06* dataset [18] such that the first seven measurements provide a performance's evaluation related to misclassified/correctly classified pixels, whereas the rest of the measurements provides a global assessment

	Video 2	Video 2 red	Video 3	Video 4	Video 5	Video 6	Video 7	Video 8
Recall	83.34	82.74	64.96	81.62	78.59	79.79	78.66	94.06
Precision	95.74	95.36	89.52	87.96	90.75	89.97	89.42	92.28
TPR	45.73	46.01	17.11	40.36	77.21	78.40	24.53	38.09
FPR	0.10	0.11	0.40	0.62	0.62	0.77	0.34	1.89
TNR	99.90	99.89	99.60	99.37	99.38	99.24	99.65	98.11
NPV	99.49	99.50	98.82	99.24	98.67	98.43	99.18	99.29
FDR	6.93	7.43	48.71	22.46	9.41	10.03	25.83	35.74
Accuracy	99.42	99.42	98.44	98.67	98.16	97.81	98.89	97.63
MCC	0.83	0.82	0.52	0.72	0.83	0.83	0.65	0.83
F1 score	0.89	0.88	0.59	0.83	0.83	0.84	0.82	0.92
JC	0.70	0.69	0.33	0.58	0.72	0.73	0.51	0.74
YC	0.92	0.92	0.76	0.78	0.89	0.89	0.73	0.82

Thus, high values for recall, precision, TPR, TNR, NPV, accuracy, MCC, F_1 score, JC and YC, and low values of FPR and FDR, result in an accurate segmentation

between the measurement values for stating a good performance of the approach, i.e., high values for measurements of the foreground pixel classification and low values for those which evaluate the background pixel tagging (see Table 3.4).

Again, the problem of lacking a *training period* free of foreground elements is considered in the *video sequence 6*. The background scene is the same as the one in the *video sequences 1, 2* and *5*, an indoor background with constant illumination conditions where one or more foreground elements are moving around. In particular, a boy is in the scene from the first captured frame, while a little girl enters and leaves the scene during the whole experiment. Again, the implemented algorithm is capable of detecting this situation such that the reference frame used in the first algorithm stage is properly updated as well as the statistical background model to be built. In that way, the initial statistical background model is only composed of background pixels as depicted in Fig. 3.14. Therefore, both target elements have been successfully detected (see Fig. 3.16 and Table 3.4 for qualitative and quantitative results respectively).

The next case of study also refers to the background oscillation problem, the different kinds of targets and the number of them. Basically, the observed scene is composed of a street where there are parked cars, swaying trees, and four elements of interest (i.e. a car, a cat, and two virtual girls) moving along the whole scene. Thus, the video sequence starts with a period without any foreground element in the scene. Then, a cat enters the scene and leaves it after crossing the street. After that, a yellow car drives from one side of the road to the other by also leaving the scene. Again, the cat appears and disappears as it previously did. Finally, two virtual girls enter the scene and move around it. As illustrated in Fig. 3.17, all the foreground elements were successfully detected regardless of their kind or their number. Nevertheless,

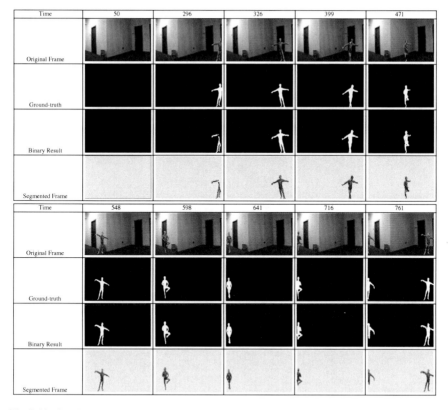

Fig. 3.11 Qualitative results for the *video sequence 2* of the *VSSN06* dataset [18] by using a reduced number of frames to build the initial background model. So, the *first row* shows the original frame of the sequence, the *second row* depicts the ground-truth frame and, the *last two rows* illustrate the segmentation result obtained by the **MoD** approach: a binary image representing the background/foreground classification carried out, such that the background is represented by *black* and the foreground pixels are coded in *white*; and a image, where the foreground elements appear as in the original frame, whereas the background is coded in an *artificial, homogeneous color*

the background vacillation again influences quantitative results, especially TPR and FDR, as shown in Table 3.4.

Finally, *video sequence 8* evaluates algorithm's performance when partial illumination changes occur. Note that it is a new problem since it is neither a gradual illumination change nor a global lightning change. Thus, first, the scene is gradually illuminated the result of which can be observed in frame 400 (see Fig. 3.18). As it is a gradual change, our approach is capable of properly dealing with it. Then, the lights are turned off. However, the illumination only changes in one part of the image, as it is highlighted in frame 594. Therefore, the global illumination change alarm is not triggered. For that reason, *false positives* are present in that area until the background model is properly updated, which again has a negative effect on

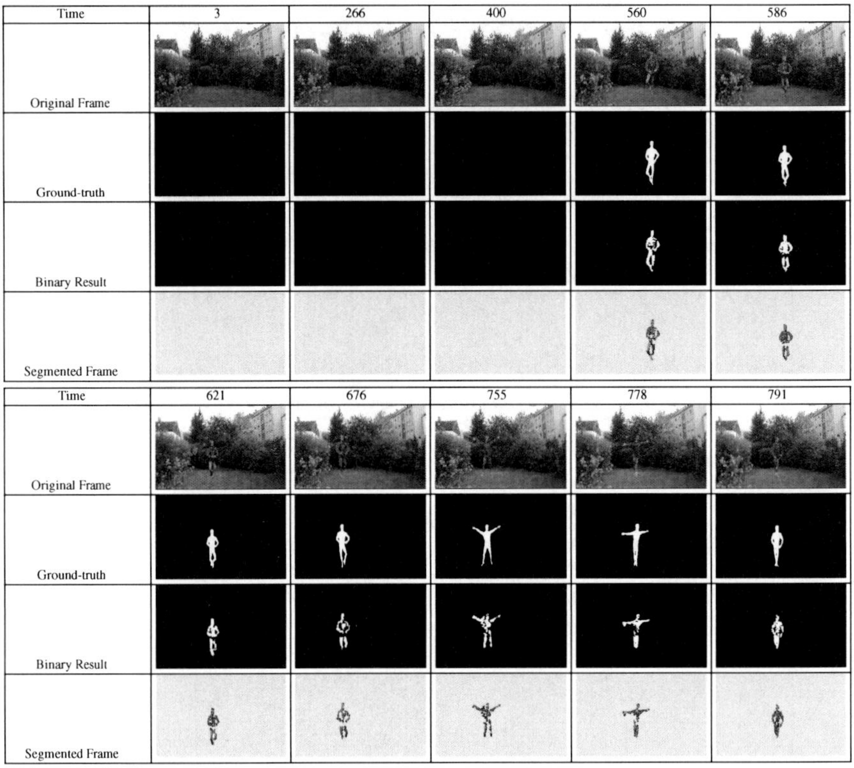

Fig. 3.12 Qualitative results for the *video sequence 3* of the *VSSN06* dataset [18], where a boy is moving around an outdoor garden with oscillating elements. Hence, the *first row* shows the original frame of the sequence, the *second row* depicts the ground-truth frame, and the *last two rows* illustrate the segmentation result obtained by the **CoD** approach: a binary image representing the background/foreground classification carried out, such that the background is represented by *black color* and the foreground pixels are coded in *white*; and a color image, where the foreground elements appear as in the original frame, whereas the background is coded in an *artificial, homogeneous color*

the quantitative results (see Table 3.4). On the contrary, after solving that issue, the segmentation is successful, even when two targets are considered.

3.3.1.3 Audiovisual People Dataset

As it was previously introduced, this dataset [19] is composed of three 8−bit AVI sequences recorded by a KOBI KF-31CD analog CCD surveillance camera in the Department of Electronic Engineering—Queen Mary University of London. Note that in this section only qualitative results are presented since no ground-truth has been provided for this dataset.

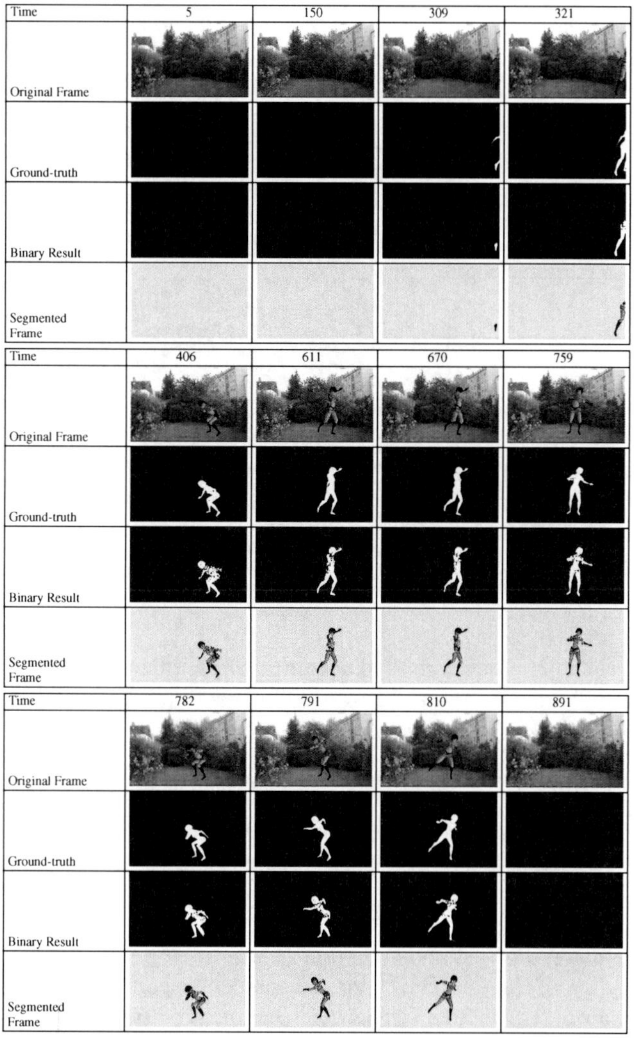

Fig. 3.13 Qualitative results for the *video sequence 4* of the *VSSN06* dataset [18], where a girl is moving around an outdoor garden with oscillating elements. Thus, the *first row* shows the original frame of the sequence, the *second row* depicts the ground-truth frame, and the *last two rows* illustrate the segmentation result obtained by the **MoD** approach: a binary image representing the background/foreground classification carried out, such that the background is represented by *black* and the foreground pixels are coded in *white*; and a color image, where the foreground elements appear as in the original frame, whereas the background is coded in an *artificial, homogeneous color*

Thus, the first video sequence considers two different segmentation problems: a *training period* with foreground elements and occlusions. With regard to the first problem, as pointed out above, the *ghosting* problem is suppressed when the

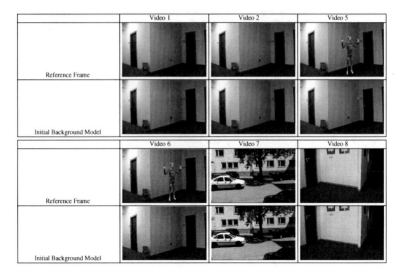

Fig. 3.14 Mean intensity for the initial background model built for all the considered video sequences of the *VSSN06* dataset [18]

algorithm is capable of detecting that situation, that is, there is no overlap between the *ghosting* blob and the actual foreground element blob. In this case, it happens when an occlusion takes place (by frame 284). Take into account that this event occurs after building the initial background model. Consequently, the person appears as part of the initial built background model as it can be observed in Fig. 3.19. Nevertheless, it is properly updated when the situation is identified such that the person to be segmented is successfully detected when he newly appears in the scene, as depicted in Fig. 3.20.

In the second instance, the influence of the target number on the algorithm's performance is studied. Two different individuals are entering and leaving the observed scene, i.e., a computer room. Therefore, the approach's performance is evaluated in different situations: (1) without targets, (2) with one person moving around and, (3) when both targets are present in the scene. A sample of the resulting segmentation is shown in Fig. 3.21. Again, a qualitative evaluation provides a good performance of our approach for different target locations as well as number of individuals.

Finally, the third video sequence evaluates the algorithm's performance in view of speed changes, i.e., two people move around the scene at different speeds. Thus, in this case, to begin with, the scene is free of foreground elements. Then, after 100 frames, the first person enters the scene, while the second one enters several frames later. They move around it, approaching and moving away from the camera, walking and running, and occluding each other sometimes. As depicted in Fig. 3.22, the qualitative results are also successful.

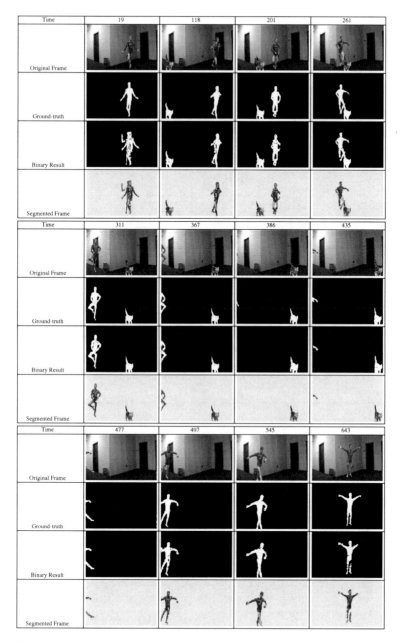

Fig. 3.15 Qualitative results for the *video sequence 5* of the *VSSN06* dataset [18], where **MoD** performance is analyzed in view of both the presence of foreground elements during the *training period* and the detection of target elements different from human beings. Thus, the *first row* shows the original frame of the sequence, the *second row* depicts the ground-truth frame and, the *last two rows* illustrate the segmentation result obtained by the **MoD** approach: a binary image representing the background/foreground classification carried out, such that the background is represented by *black color* and the foreground pixels are coded in *white*; and a color image, where the foreground elements appear as in the original frame, whereas the background is coded in an *artificial, homogeneous color*

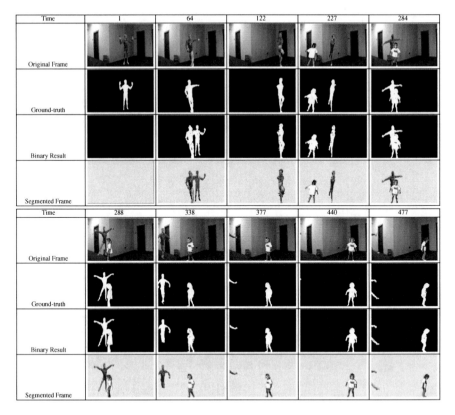

Fig. 3.16 Qualitative results for the *video sequence 6* of the *VSSN06* dataset [18], where the problem of lacking a *training period* free of foreground elements is considered. So, the *first row* shows the original frame of the sequence, the *second row* depicts the ground-truth frame and, the *last two rows* illustrate the segmentation result obtained by the **MoD** approach: a binary image representing the background/foreground classification carried out, such that the background is represented by *black color* and the foreground pixels are coded in *white*; and a color image, where the foreground elements appear as in the original frame, whereas the background is coded in an *artificial, homogeneous color*

3.3.2 Experimental Results Over Our Own Dataset

In this section, we evaluate the approach's performance over images taken by two different kinds of imaging devices. So, first, results obtained over perspective images are presented. Then, the **MoD**'s performance is assessed over fisheye images.

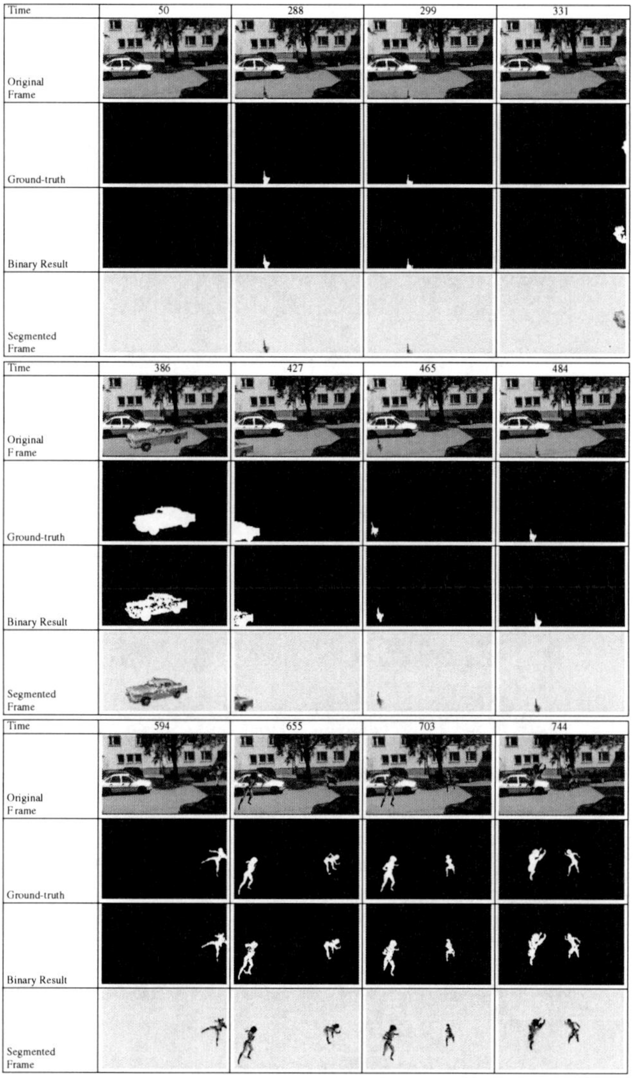

Fig. 3.17 Qualitative results for the *video sequence 7* of the *VSSN06* dataset [18], where the observed scene is composed of a street where there are parked cars, swaying trees, and four elements of interest (i.e. a car, a cat, and two virtual girls) moving along the whole scene. Thus, the *first row* shows the original frame of the sequence, the *second row* depicts the ground-truth frame, and the *last two rows* illustrate the segmentation result obtained by the **MoD** approach: a binary image representing the background/foreground classification carried out, such that the background is represented by *black color* and the foreground pixels are coded in *white*; and a color image, where the foreground elements appear as in the original frame, whereas the background is coded in an *artificial, homogeneous color*

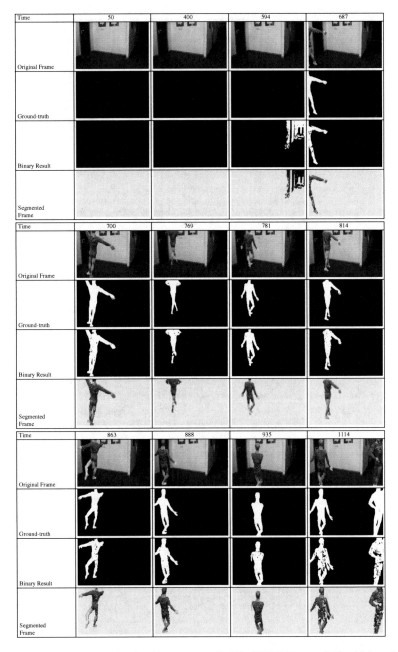

Fig. 3.18 Qualitative results for the *video sequence 8* of the *VSSN06* dataset [18], which evaluates algorithm performance when partial illumination changes occur. Thus, the *first row* shows the original frame of the sequence, the *second row* depicts the ground-truth frame and, the *last two rows* illustrate the segmentation result obtained by the **MoD** approach: a binary image representing the background/foreground classification carried out, such that the background is represented by *black color* and the foreground pixels are coded in *white*; and a color image, where the foreground elements appear as in the original frame, whereas the background is coded in an *artificial, homogeneous color*

Fig. 3.19 Mean intensity for the initial background model built for all the video sequences of the *Audiovisual People Dataset* [19]

3.3.2.1 Perspective Image Experiments

As it was introduced in the previous chapter, the experiments carried out consist of analyzing images taken by one lens of a *STH-DCSG Stereo head* [29]. Again, both *monochrome* and images with different resolution are considered.

In the first experiment, the camera was located at one side of our laboratory room. A person is continuously entering and leaving the scene such that different situations can be studied such as occlusions or target motionless. Qualitative results are depicted in Fig. 3.23. Note that the segmentation is more accurate than the one presented in the previous chapter.

With regard to the *monochrome* images, the same image sequence as in the previous chapter is analyzed. Basically, it consists of observing a scene of our laboratory room where a person is entering and leaving, while different changes in illumination occur. Moreover, the problem of distinguishing between a foreground object that becomes motionless and a background object that moves and then becomes motionless, is also studied. Thus, in the first part of the experiment, depicted in the first row of Fig. 3.25, a person enters the scene where lights are switched on. The difficulty in this image sequence lies on the high pixel brightness since it provides less differences in pixel values. Then, a global illumination change takes place. Again, the person enters the scene, and moves around. Note that her proximity to the camera does not trigger a false lightning change. Furthermore, the person moves a chair, which is part of the current background, to a new position. As it can be seen in Fig. 3.25 (frame 1461), the chair was initially considered as foreground together with the target person. Later, lights are completely turned off by obtaining a scene with really poor illumination. Even in those conditions, the proposed approach is capable of detecting the person. In addition, in order to evaluate the algorithm's performance when a foreground element temporarily stops, the person sits in the moved chair and remains in that position during more than 200 frames (from frame 2040 to 2235) and she is properly detected in all of them. Finally, two more global illumination changes

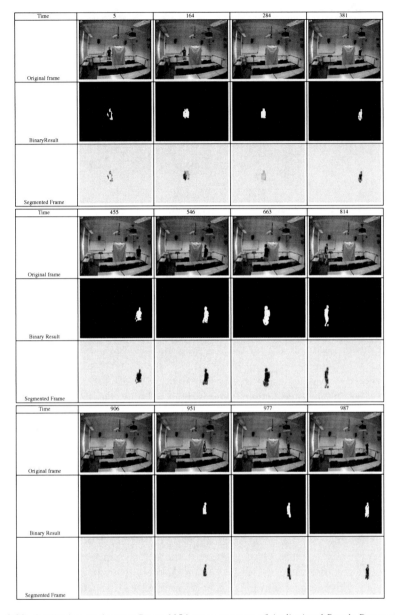

Fig. 3.20 Qualitative results over *Room 105* image sequence of *Audiovisual People Dataset* [19], where a person is moving around a classroom. Thus, the *first row* of each block shows the original frame of the sequence, whereas the *last two rows* illustrate the segmentation result obtained by the **MoD** approach: a binary image representing the background/foreground classification carried out, such that the background is represented by *black color* and the foreground pixels are coded in *white*; and a color image, where the foreground elements appear as in the original frame, whereas the background is coded in an *artificial, homogeneous color*

Fig. 3.21 Qualitative results over *Room 160* video sequence of *Audiovisual People Dataset* [19], where two people are moving around a computer room. Thus, the *first row* of each group shows the original frame of the sequence, whereas the *last two rows* illustrate the segmentation result obtained by the **MoD** approach: a binary image representing the background/foreground classification carried out, such that the background is represented by *black color* and the foreground pixels are coded in *white*; and a color image, where the foreground elements appear as in the original frame, whereas the background is coded in an *artificial, homogeneous color*

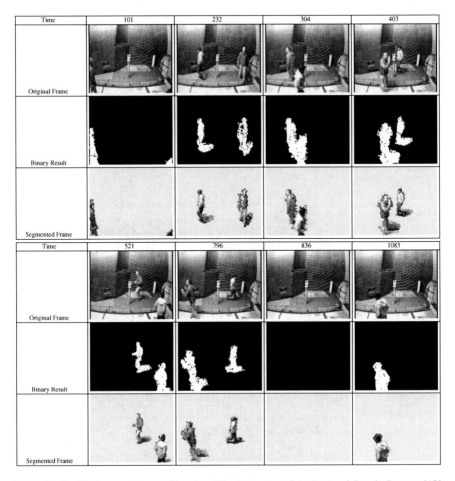

Fig. 3.22 Qualitative results over *Chamber* video sequence of *Audiovisual People Dataset* [19], where two people are continuously entering and leaving a room with reduced reverberations. Thus, the *first row* of each group shows the original frame of the sequence, whereas the *last two rows* illustrate the segmentation result obtained by the **MoD** approach: a binary image representing the background/foreground classification carried out, such that the background is represented by *black color* and the foreground pixels are coded in *white*; and a color image, where the foreground elements appear as in the original frame, whereas the background is coded in an *artificial, homogeneous color*

occur, but, unlike the previous one, they have used to gradually brighten the scene. In all the cases, the target person is successfully segmented by properly adapting the background model to all those dynamic factors which can influence the segmentation result. As a sample, Fig. 3.24 shows the temporal sequence of the mean intensity background model after each illumination change.

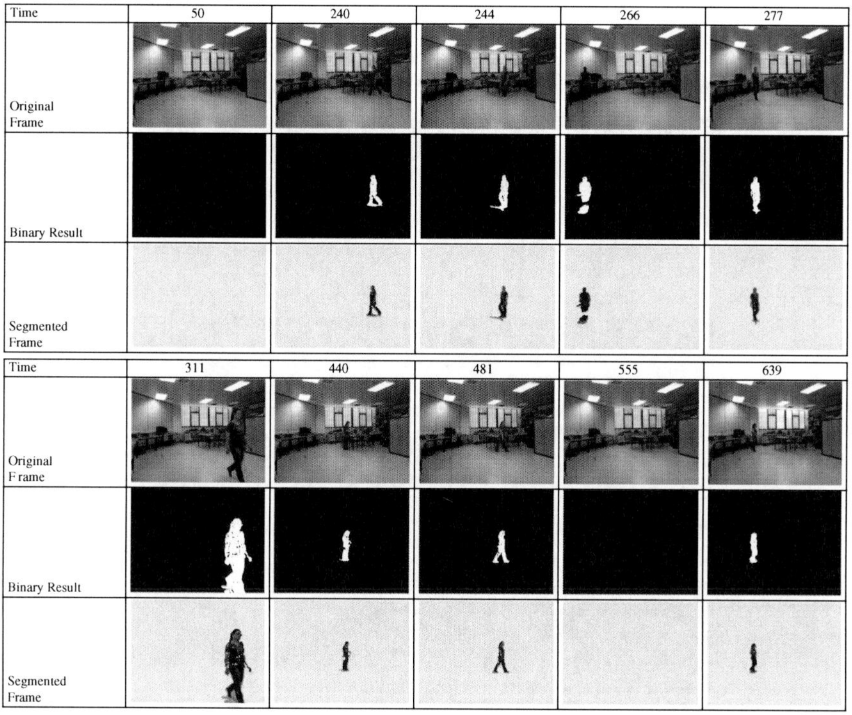

Time	50	240	244	266	277
Original Frame					
Binary Result					
Segmented Frame					
Time	311	440	481	555	639
Original Frame					
Binary Result					
Segmented Frame					

Fig. 3.23 Qualitative results over perspective images such that a person is continuously entering and leaving our laboratory room. Thus, the *first row* shows the original frame of the sequence, whereas the *last two rows* illustrate the segmentation result obtained by the **MoD** approach: a binary image representing the background/foreground classification carried out, such that the background is represented by *black color* and the foreground pixels are coded in *white*; and a color image, where the foreground elements appear as in the original frame, whereas the background is coded in an *artificial, homogeneous color*

Fig. 3.24 Background model evolution after each illumination change by means of its mean intensity

3.3.2.2 Fisheye Image Experiments

The next experiment deals with global changes in illumination. For that, a *SSC-DC330P* third-inch camera was used [30]. It is equipped with an on-chip lens structure with a microlens over each pixel on its CCD by dramatically improving camera sensitivity. Furthermore, the new cell of ExwaveHAD technology minimizes the

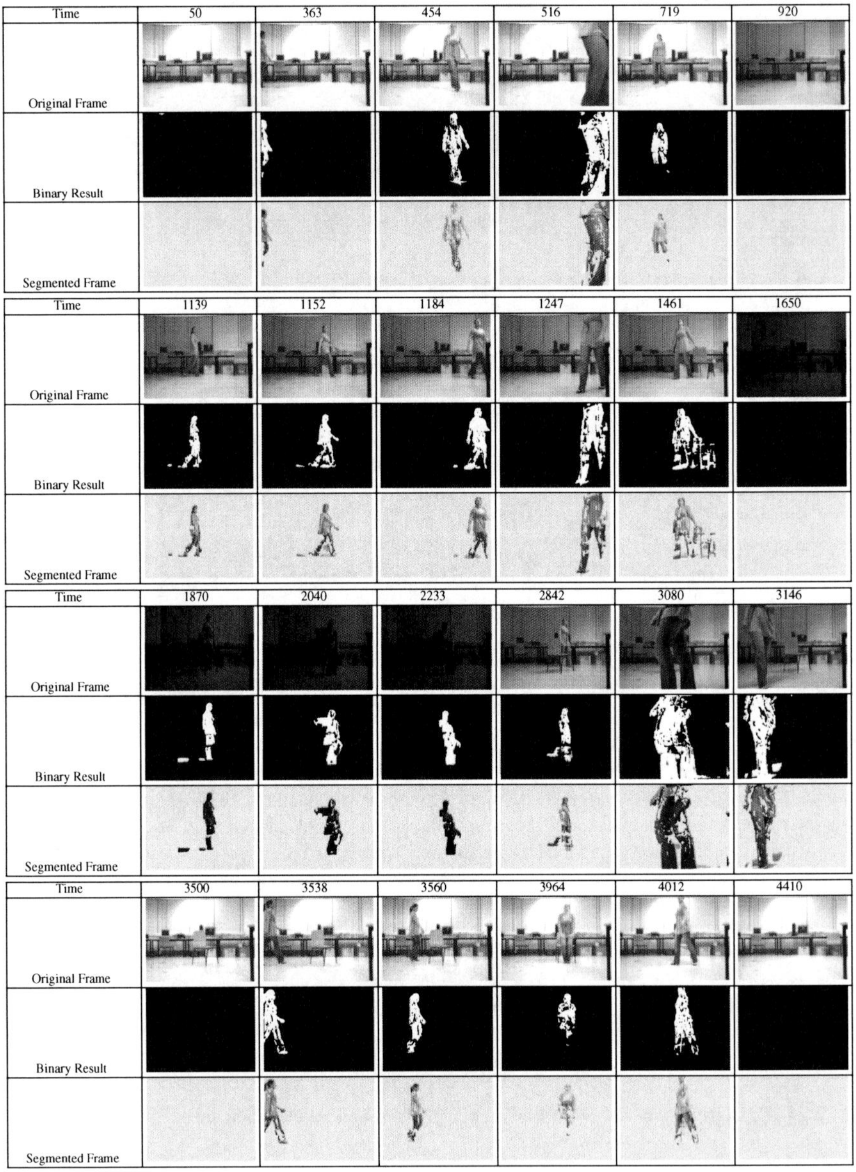

Time	50	363	454	516	719	920
Original Frame						
Binary Result						
Segmented Frame						
Time	1139	1152	1184	1247	1461	1650
Original Frame						
Binary Result						
Segmented Frame						
Time	1870	2040	2233	2842	3080	3146
Original Frame						
Binary Result						
Segmented Frame						
Time	3500	3538	3560	3964	4012	4410
Original Frame						
Binary Result						
Segmented Frame						

Fig. 3.25 Qualitative results over grayscale perspective images such that a person is continuously entering and leaving our laboratory room. Thus, the *first row* shows the original frame of the sequence, whereas the *last two rows* illustrate the segmentation result obtained by the **MoD** approach: a binary image representing the background/foreground classification carried out, such that the background is represented by *black color* and the foreground pixels are coded in *white*; and a color image, where the foreground elements appear as in the original frame, whereas the background is coded in an *artificial, homogeneous color*

Table 3.5 Parameter values used for fisheye images when the **MoD** is performed

	10°
	15 pix
Subimage Size	
Erosion Mask	0 1 0 0 1 1 0 0 0
Dilation Mask	1 1 1 1 1 1 1 1 1

reflexion of unwanted light within the CCD by reducing the suffered smear level; and increases spectrum length in the near-infrared wavelength area of 700–1000 nm. Therefore, it also improves the sensibility of the camera and makes it possible to produce images at a low light level (up to 0.8 lux with F1.2 lens, 50 IRE video level). The set of the algorithm parameters used in the following experiments is summarized in Table 3.5.

Thus, the fisheye camera is located at the center of our laboratory room such that the number of people in the scene changes along time. However, the proposed approach properly identifies their presence in the scene, as shown in Fig. 3.26. As depicted, the individuals to be detected are a boy and a girl and they continuously enter and leave the scene.

Then, we present another experiment where a person is entering and leaving the scene, while several lightning changes take place. First, lights are switched off, later they are turned on in order to finally be off again. Frames shown in Fig. 3.27 try to be representative of all the obtained results. As it can be observed, qualitative results highlight the **MoD**'s good performance.

To conclude this section, a runtime analysis is performed. Figure 3.28 shows the results obtained for the same image sequence at different scales when the C++ implementation of the both proposed algorithms up to now (**MoD** and **CoD**) were run on an Intel(R) Core(TM) Duo CPU P8700 at 2.53 GHz. It can be observed that insignificant differences exist when the image size is small, whereas, as the image size gets larger, the runtime quickly increases for the **MoD** approach. It is because a larger image implies a higher background model and a higher number of Gaussian distributions being continuously updated. Even so, a real-time execution is obtained with a 320×240 image resolution.

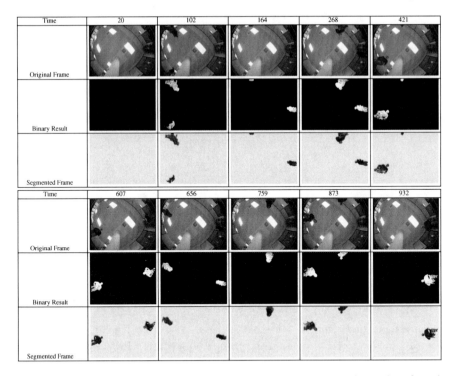

Fig. 3.26 Qualitative results for fisheye images for a video sequence where the number of people in the scene changes along time. Thus, the *first row* shows the original frame of the sequence, whereas the *last two rows* illustrate the segmentation result obtained by the **MoD** approach: a binary image representing the background/foreground classification carried out, such that the background is represented by *black color* and the foreground pixels are coded in *white*; and a color image, where the foreground elements appear as in the original frame, whereas the background is coded in an *artificial, homogeneous color*

3.4 Conclusions

Motion detection is the core of multiple automated visual applications by providing a stimulus to detect objects of interest in the field of view of the sensor. Such detection is usually carried out by using Background Subtraction (BS) methods, especially for applications relying on a fixed camera. Basically, the idea behind these kinds of techniques is to first build a background model from a sequence of images in order to find the interest objects from the difference between that background estimation and the current frame. Therefore, the accuracy of the segmentation process depends on how well the background is modeled.

Despite the wide research done in this area, there are still some problems that have not been addressed by most BS algorithms. Among them, we can find the quick illumination changes, the proper update of the background model when a

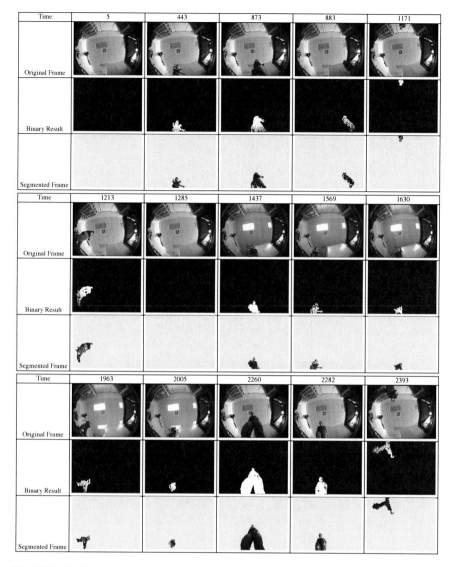

Fig. 3.27 Qualitative results for fisheye images for a video sequence where several lightning changes take place. Thus, the *first row* shows the original frame of the sequence, whereas the *last two rows* illustrate the segmentation result obtained by the **MoD** approach: a binary image representing the background/foreground classification carried out, such that the background is represented by *black color* and the foreground pixels are coded in *white*; and a color image, where the foreground elements appear as in the original frame, whereas the background is coded in an *artificial, homogeneous color*

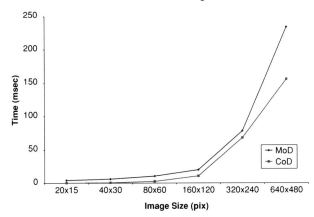

Fig. 3.28 Execution time evolution based on image size as well as the used algorithm (**MoD** and **CoD**) generated by an Intel(R) Core(TM) Duo CPU P8700 at 2.53 GHz

background object is relocated, the initialization of the background estimation when moving objects are present in the scenes, or the shadows.

In this chapter, motion detection in real-life scenarios has been studied. For that, the estimated model should properly describe the scene background which can change due to the presence of moving background objects (e.g. swaying vegetation, fluctuating water, flickering monitors, ascending escalators, etc.), camera oscillations, changes in illumination (gradual or sudden) or in the background geometry such as parked cars, and so on.

With the aim of dealing with those challenges, we have presented a novel, sensor-independent background subtraction technique, the **MoD**, which is robust and generic enough to handle the complexities of most natural dynamic scenes. Basically, it is composed of two different stages. The first one is to build a reliable, statistical background model but considering the possibility that foreground objects can be present. Thus, constraints like waiting for a period of time to build the initial background, do not exist since a segmentation process is carried out with a mixture of two difference techniques (i.e. using the **CoD** approach). In the second stage, a motion detection as well as a proper background update have been carried out. For that, a mixture of three difference approaches is used: *temporal adjacent frame difference*, *background(-frame) subtraction* and *background maintenance*. Thus, the raw pixel classification obtained by the **CoD** approach, is improved by means of a background subtraction using the statistical background model built in the previous stage and updated along time. Moreover, a sudden illumination change detection technique is incorporated in both stages to properly adapt the system to it.

In addition, the algorithm's performance has been tested over two different kinds of images: ones taken by a perspective camera and ones taken by a dioptric sensor. With regard to the perspective images, two different types of experiments were carried out. Thus, on the one hand, three public image datasets designed to test and compare different background maintenance algorithms were used. In that way, it has been demonstrated that our approach outperforms previous well-known techniques for which results are available. On the other hand, it was also run in real scenarios by means of a camera. In addition, good performance results were obtained when fisheye images were considered.

Finally, a time-execution analysis has been presented. In that study, two different parameters were considered: image size and the used algorithm (**MoD** and **CoD**). It highlights that insignificant differences between the two approaches (i.e. **MoD** and **CoD**) in terms of execution time, exist when the image size is small, whereas, as the image size gets larger, the runtime quickly increases when **MoD** is used since it has to deal with a higher background model and a higher number of Gaussian distributions continuously updated. Even so, a real-time execution is obtained with a 320 × 240 image resolution. Consequently, the proposed approach can be used for real-time robotic tasks.

References

1. Heikkila, J., Silve, O.: A real-time system for monitoring of cyclists and pedestrians.: Second IEEE Workshop on Visual Surveillance, pp. 74–81. Fort Collins, Colorado (1999)
2. Cavallaro, A., Ebrahimi, T.: Video object extraction based on adaptive background and statistical change detection. In: B. Girod, C.A. Bouman, E.G. Steinbach (eds.) Visual Communications and Image Processing 2001, pp. 465–475. SPIE (2000)
3. Lee, B., Hedley, M.: Background estimation for video surveillance. In: Image and Vision Computing New Zealand (IVCNZ), pp. 315–320. Auckland, New Zealand (2005)
4. Gloyer, B., Aghajan, H., Siu, K.Y., Kailath, T.: Video-based freeway-monitoring system using recursive vehicle tracking. In: SPIE Annual Meeting, pp. 173–180. San Jose, CA, USA (1995)
5. Massey, M., Bender, W.: Salient stills: process and practice. IBM Systems Journal **35**(3–4), 557–573 (1996)
6. Lo, B., Velastin, S.: Automatic congestion detection system for underground platforms. In: International Symposium on Intelligent Multimedia, Video and Speech Processing, pp. 158–161. Kowloon Shangri-La, Hong Kong, China (2001)
7. Zhou, Q., Aggarwal, J.: Tracking and classifying moving objects from video. In: Second IEEE Workshop on Performance Evaluation of Tracking and Surveillance (PETS). Kauai, Hawai (2001)
8. Cucchiara, R., Grana, C., Piccardi, M., Prati, A.: Detecting moving objects, ghosts, and shadows in video streams. IEEE Transactions on Pattern Analysis and Machine Intelligence (PAMI) **25**(10), 1337–1342 (2003)
9. Elgammal, A., Harwood, D., Davis, L.: Background and foreground modeling using non-parametric kernel density estimation for visual surveillance. In: IEEE Proceedings, pp. 1151–1163 (2002)
10. Collins, R., Lipton, A., Kanade, T., Fijiyoshi, H., Duggins, D., Tsin, Y., Tolliver, D., Enomoto, N., Hasegawa, O., Burt, P., Wixson, L.: A system for video surveillance and monitoring. Tech. rep., Carnegie Mellon University, Pittsburg, PA (2000)
11. Kanade, T., Collins, R., Lipton, A., Burt, P., Wixson, L.: Advances in cooperative multi-sensor video surveillance. In: Darpa Image Understanding Workshop, vol. I, pp. 3–24. Morgan Kaufmann (1998)

12. Wren, C., Azarbeyejani, A., Darrell, T., Pentland, A.: Pfinder: Real-time tracking of the human body. IEEE Transactions on Pattern Analysis and Machine Intelligence (PAMI) **19**(7), 780–785 (1997)
13. Azarbayejani, A., Wren, C., Pentland, A.: Real-time 3-d tracking of the human body. In: IMAGE'COM, 374. Bordeaux, France (1996)
14. Stauffer, C., Grimson, W.: Learning patterns of activity using real-time tracking. IEEE Transactions on Pattern Analysis and Machine Intelligence (PAMI) **27**(5), 747–757 (2000).
15. Gao, X., Boult, T., Coetzee, F., Ramesh, V.: Error analysis of background subtraction. In: IEEE International Conference on Computer Vision and Pattern Recognition (CVPR), pp. 1503–1510. Hilton Head, SC, USA (2000)
16. Benezeth, Y., Jodoin, P., Emile, B., Laurent, H., Rosenberger, C.: Review and evaluation of commonly-implemented background subtraction algorithms. In: 19th International Conference on Pattern Recognition (ICPR), pp. 1–4. Tampa, Florida (2008)
17. Toyama, K., Krumm, J., Brumitt, B.: http://research.microsoft.com/en-us/um/people/jckrumm/WallFlower/TestImages.htm (1999)
18. Hörster, E., Lienhart, R.: http://mmc36.informatik.uni-augsburg.de/VSSN06_OSAC/ (2006)
19. Taj, M.: Surveillance performance evaluation initiative (spevi)—audiovisual people dataset. http://www.elec.qmul.ac.uk/staffinfo/andrea/avss2007_d.html (2007)
20. Stauffer, C., Grimson, W.: Adaptive background mixture models for real-time tracking. In: IEEE Conference on Computer Vision and Pattern Recognition (CVPR), pp. 246–252 (1999).
21. Matsuyama, T., Ohya, T., Habe, H.: Background subtraction for non-stationary scenes. In: Fourth Asian Conference on Computer Vision, pp. 662–667. Singapore (2000)
22. Haritaoglu, I., Harwood, D., Davis, L.: W4: Real-time surveillance of people and their activities. IEEE Transactions on Pattern Analysis and Machine Intelligence (PAMI) **22**(8), 809–830 (2000)
23. Nakai, H.: Non-parameterized bayes decision method for moving object detection. In: Asian Conference on Computer Vision. Singapore (1995)
24. Oliver, N., Rosario, B., Pentland, A.: A bayesian computer vision system for modeling human interactions. IEEE Transactions on Pattern Analysis and Machine Intelligence (PAMI) **22**(8), 831–843 (2000)
25. Toyama, K., Krum, J., Brumitt, B., Meyers, B.: Wallflower: Principles and practice of background maintenance. In: Seventh IEEE International Conference on Computer Vision (ICCV), vol. 1, pp. 255–261. Kerkyra, Greece (1999)
26. Kottow, D., Koppen, M., del Solar, J.R.: A background maintenance model in the spatial-range domain. In: 2nd ECCV Workshop on Statistical Methods in Video Processing, pp. 141–152. Prague, Czech Republic (2004)
27. Varcheie, P., Sills-Lavoie, M., Bilodeau, G.A.: An efficient region-based background subtraction technique. In: Canadian Conference on Computer and Robot Vision, pp. 71–78 (2008)
28. Migliore, D., Matteucci, M., Naccari, M.: A revaluation of frame difference in fast and robust motion detection. In: 4th ACM International Workshop on Video Surveillance and Sensor Networks (VSSN), pp. 215–218. Santa Barbara, California (2006)
29. VidereDesign: http://198.144.193.48/index.php?id=31
30. Sony: http://www.infodip.com/pages/sony/camera/pdf/SSC-DC58AP.pdf

Chapter 4
Applications

Abstract Motion detection is of widespread interest due to a large number of applications in various disciplines such as, for instance, video surveillance [1–4], remote sensing [5–8], medical diagnosis and treatment [9–11], civil infrastructure [12–14], underwater sensing [15–17], objective measures of intervention effectiveness in team sports [18], and driver assistance system [19–21], to name some. Among the diversity, some real applications have been implemented to evaluate approach's performance. These real applications as well as their performance results are presented and discussed through this chapter.

Keywords Machine vision · Computer vision · Image segmentation · Background subtraction · Motion detection · Robot vision · Dynamic environments · Visual surveillance · Applications · Real applications · Human bahavior analysis · Visual activity monitoring

4.1 Biological Studies

4.1.1 Introduction

Behavior is one of the most important properties of animal's life because it allows animals to interact with their environment as well as other organisms. With the aim of understanding the causes, functions, development, and evolution of behavior, biologists try to answer one or more of the four questions to model the animal behavior proposed by Tinbergen [22]. Basically, the first question asks about the mechanisms of a behavior. That is, what stimulates an animal to respond with the behavior it displays and what the response mechanisms are. The second question concerns the translation of genotype to phenotype. In other words, as an individual grows from an embryo to an adult, there are developmental processes which allow the implementation of mature behaviors in their organism. The third question deals

E. Martínez-Martín and A. P. del Pobil, *Robust Motion Detection in Real-Life Scenarios*,
SpringerBriefs in Computer Science, DOI: 10.1007/978-1-4471-4216-4_4,
© Ester Martínez-Martín 2012

with the function of a particular behavior in order to be successful in a specific task. Finally, the last question examines the evolutionary history of a behavior along time, from ancestors up to the current species.

The first two questions are proximate questions, i.e., they are the **how** questions, while the last two questions involve evolutionary and historical thinking: these are the **why** questions. However, answering these questions implies to solve a wider range of issues such as how animals communicate, how neural mechanisms control behavior, why animals are altruistic to family members, why some animals look after their off-spring whereas others do not, or why species differ in their mating systems. So, research on animal behavior and behavioral ecology has taken a number of forms. Here, we have focused on the study of individual animal behavior.

4.1.2 Animal Communication Analysis

Most animal communication is multimodal that implies a complete examination of multiple signal channels, such as audio and vision, in order to achieve a complete understanding of their behavior. For that, field observation, video playbacks, and their subsequent processing must be carried out. However, note that the required processing can become a tedious, difficult task when the amount of data to be analyzed is high. As a solution, an autonomous surveillance system can be used.

In this section, we present a work developed in collaboration with Sarah Partan from the Hampshire College [23], aimed at studying the behavior of a dewlap lizard. Mainly, a dewlap lizard is a reptile which has large skin dewlaps under its neck, such that it can extend and retract those dewlaps. The dewlaps are usually of a different color from the rest of its body and can be enlarged to make the lizard seem much bigger than it really is, specially when warding off predators. Thus, the males use the dewlap to intimidate rivals and also to attract females during mating season. Despite the male dewlap lizard is much larger in size, the female anoles do indeed possess a dewlap as well. These uses for the dewlap work much in the same way as the neck frill on a frill-necked lizard, with the lizard extending its neck frill for much of the same reasons. Nevertheless, it is not known if the dewlap is used in thermo regulation like the neck frill is.

Therefore, our experiment consists of processing a video playback of a dewlap lizard by aiming at detecting its two mechanisms for communication: its movement up-down and the extraction and/or retraction of its dewlap. Figure 4.1 illustrates some of the obtained results on the same image sequence. As it might be observed, the up-down movement of the dewlap lizard is detected by the whole body, while only the dewlap is marked when it is extracted or retracted.

It is worth noting that it is a difficult task since the dewlap shown in the images is almost transparent due to the bright scene, which makes it more difficult to be detected. However, it could be easily detected in other scenarios such as, for instance, the second experiment depicted in Fig. 4.2. Basically, this experiment presents a video sequence in which a dewlap is continuously extracting and retracting its dewlap. In

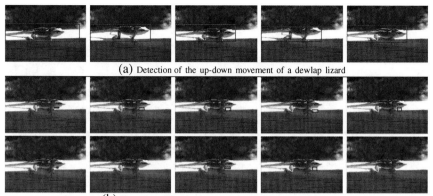

(a) Detection of the up-down movement of a dewlap lizard

(b) Detection of the dewlap extraction and/or retractaction

Fig. 4.1 Detection of the two dewlap lizard mechanisms for communication by using the **MoD** approach. **a** Detection of the up-down movement of a dewlap lizard. **b** Detection of the dewlap extraction and/or retraction

this case, the movement up-down is not carried out, although the movement of its head and the shake of the camera make the detection more difficult. So, unlike the camera shake, solved by properly adjusting the parameters of the algorithm, a post-processing method is applied in order to deal with the head movement. In this case, a color filter has been applied on the potential foreground pixels. Note that the postprocess is only necessary when the head movement is done, that is, in the early frames, since the results obtained by the proposed algorithm are successful otherwise. So, Fig. 4.2b shows the results of applying the color filter only to the problematic frames since the other results are the same.

4.2 Traffic Flow Monitoring

Other application can be the traffic flow monitoring and the traffic analysis since they can be modeled as surveillance systems. So, the resulting video images could be used to estimate traffic flows, detect vehicles, and pedestrians for signal timing, and track vehicles and pedestrians for safety applications. Technically these systems are based on stationary video cameras as well as computers connected to wide area networks. Their aim is to detect pedestrians, vehicles, or both of them, for long hours in all weather conditions and at any time of the day. So, the designed vision system can be used for detecting and reporting speed violations or traffic congestions as well as for triggering an alarm when an accident happens or someone shows a *suspicious* behavior. Although some examples of this kind of applications can be found in the literature [24–27], most of them do not fit to real-time road monitoring processes.

Here, we present some of the results obtained for the publicly available image data set [28]. We analyze a set of traffic sequences showing the intersection Karl-Wilhelm-/Berthold-Strae in Karlsruhe. Its gray-scale/color images were

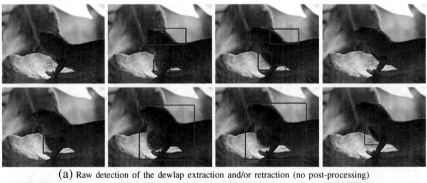

(a) Raw detection of the dewlap extraction and/or retraction (no post-processing)

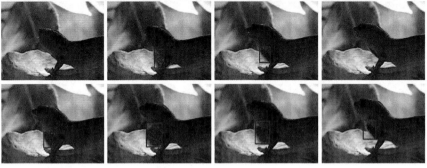

(b) Detection of the dewlap extraction and/or retractaction with a post-processing method

Fig. 4.2 Detection of the dewlap extraction and/or retraction by using the **MoD** approach. **a** Raw detection of the dewlap extraction and/or retraction (no postprocessing). **b** Detection of the dewlap extraction and/or retraction with a postprocessing method

recorded by a stationary camera with a 768 × 576 resolution. As a real street is observed, there are no frames without foreground elements. Moreover, two different kinds of targets have to be detected: pedestrians and vehicles. Experimental results under different weather conditions are depicted in Figs. 4.3, 4.4, 4.5 and 4.6. Note that all the detected targets are enclosed in a red rectangle, which corresponds to their minimum bounding rectangle, by showing the identified moving elements but without applying a tracking process. It is worth noting that there are some targets that appear divided into two different parts when a partial occlusion takes place due to a lamppost or tree branches, for instance. This issue could be solved by incorporating a postprocessing to the system.

So, the first two traffic sequences monitor the intersection under normal weather conditions. Figure 4.3 shows a tram crossing the image from the right down corner to the left top one. At the same time, some pedestrians are moving at different places in the image as well as some cars. As it can be observed, all the targets were successfully identified. Something similar happens with the second sequence (see Fig. 4.4). Several cars appear in the scene and stop at a traffic light, meanwhile another set of vehicles and pedestrians are moving in other lanes. Again, a proper detection was carried out.

Fig. 4.3 Results of traffic flow monitoring under normal weather conditions obtained by the **MoD** approach

Now, the traffic monitoring task is studied when there is snow on lanes. So, the background model will be composed of both street and snow. Moreover, in this video sequence, it starts to weakly snow and the algorithm has to be capable of properly labeling those pixels as background. Figure 4.5 depicts the obtained results. As it can be observed, the detection was successful and no false positives appeared.

The last traffic sequence analyzes the results provided when there is a heavy fog. Images are considerably blurred by the fog (see Fig. 4.6) which makes the detection task difficult in some areas of the image, specially those on the top. In those areas, sometimes, the algorithm cannot distinguish between certain cars and the street. However, the results were successful.

4.3 Human Action Recognition

4.3.1 Introduction

Recognizing human action is a key component in many computer vision applications, such as video surveillance, human-computer interfaces, video indexing and browsing, recognition of gestures, human body animation, analysis of sports events, posture and gait analysis for training athletes and physically challenged people, and dance choreography.

Stating the problem in simple terms, given a sequence of images with one or more people performing an activity, can a system be designed to automatically recognize the activity being or was performed? As simple as the question seems, detecting human actions from video is a very challenging problem. The reason lies on the physical body motion can look very different depending on the context: (1) similar actions with different clothes, or in different illumination and background can result in a large appearance variation; (2) the same actions performed by two different

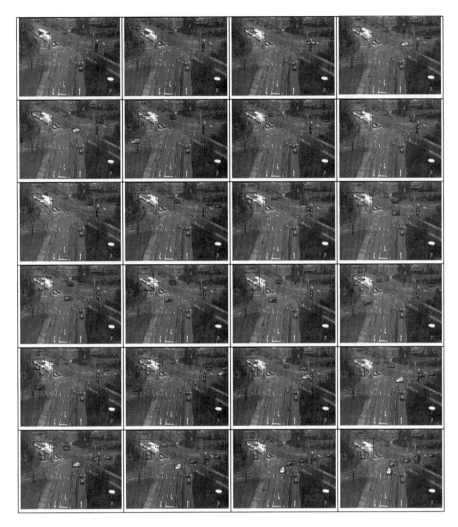

Fig. 4.4 Results of traffic flow monitoring on another traffic sequence under normal weather conditions obtained by the **MoD** approach

people can look dissimilar in terms of action speed or frame rate of the video. In addition, it should be taken into account that the designed system for that purpose has to deal, in real-time, with a wide variety of situations and conditions such as, for example, a place where illumination can be very poor at a certain time of the day, or a very populated scenario where continuous occlusions can hamper the detection process.

In recent years, this problem has caught the attention of researchers from industry, academia, security agencies, consumer agencies, and the general populace, too. They have made an effort to model and recognize human actions from different

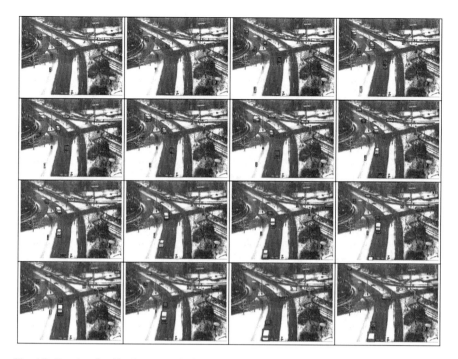

Fig. 4.5 Results of traffic flow control when there is snow on lanes obtained by the **MoD** approach

points of view, although it is broadly carried out by means of parametric time-series approaches, frame-by-frame non-parametric approaches and volumetric approaches [29]. Refer to [30–33] for detailed surveys and references therein for a good summary.

So, as Turaga et al. [33] pointed out, real-life activity recognition systems typically follow a hierarchical approach. At the lower levels there are modules such as background/foreground segmentation, tracking, and object detection. At the mid-level action-recognition modules appear. At the high level, it is required the reasoning engines that encode the activity semantics based on the lower level action primitives. Thus, the proposed algorithm in this manuscript perfectly fits for extraction of low-level image features.

4.3.2 Sports Video Analysis

Efforts at athlete motion tracking have traditionally involved a range of data collection techniques from live observation to post-event video analysis where athlete movement patterns are manually recorded and categorized to determine performance effectiveness, planning tactics and strategies, measuring team organization, providing meaningful kinematic feedback, or objective measures of intervention effectiveness

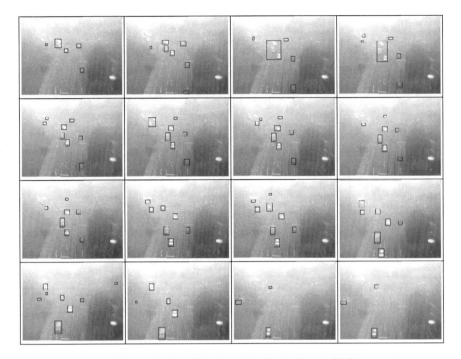

Fig. 4.6 Results of traffic monitoring with a heavy fog obtained by the **MoD** approach

in team sports, which could benefit coaches, players, and sports scientists. However, that is very time-consuming. Therefore, an automatic analysis of sports videos is desired such that it enables to evaluate the performance and/or the strategy of a team and of an individual player during training and/or official games, to automatically summarize the highlight scenes of a long sports event, or to generate a virtual view from arbitrary viewpoints.

So, the goal of the sports video analysis is to extract semantics from a source video and intelligently edit, enhance, and adapt the sports video content to various applications such as, for instance, behavior inference from the object shape [34, 35], synthesis of new views in a $3D$ reconstruction [36], or knowing the load on soccer players during a match [37, 38].

The research in the aspect of human motion capturing during sport events (training or games) has begun relatively as early as mid- 1920s. At that time, researchers like Hill [39], and later Keller [40], developed dynamic models of athletes that were used to predict the world records for linear races, such as 100 m sprint. As technology progressed, high-accuracy measurement devices were developed and they allowed researchers to study the biomechanical properties of the athletes' body as, for instance, Richards, who presented a comparison between some commercially available systems [41]. The devices in those systems were able to measure only the local features of the human body such as the positions of the extremities. So, the analysis of athletes' performance in larger scale was not possible using those systems. As a consequence, the early research has been focused on obtaining the positions of the acting elements (e.g., the position of the players and/or the ball in sports such as soccer or tennis; or the shape and movement of the athletes in other sports like gymnastics or diving) which would allow the experts to analyze the tactical behavior or performance of certain players or the whole team. For example, in Pers et al. [42] a system specifically designed to track players in squash matches enabled Vuèkoviè et al. [43] to determine the behavioral features that distinguished the loser from the winner based on the position information. The system proposed in Pers et al. [42] was further developed to track handball players and called SAGIT [44].

To that aim, the first challenge to be solved is to obtain appropriate video sequences that can robustly identify and label people over time, in a cluttered environment containing multiple interacting people. This issue often implies to deal with multiple-target management, the relative size and occlusion frequency of people, and changes in illumination. Those problems are some of the considered problems in our proposed motion detection and tracking algorithm. Consequently, our algorithm's performance has been evaluated by means of a sports video sequence. The goal is the extraction of low-level image features, i.e., foreground-background segmentation. Some of the obtained results are depicted in Fig. 4.7. As it can be seen, the football players were succesfully identified in all the images, even when they were far from the camera. Furthermore, the ball was also identified in all the images it appears. In this case, all the moving identified elements have been enclosed in a red rectangle, since no further processing has been applied. Nevertheless, in the case the goal was analyzing the behavior of one of the teams, for instance, a postprocess (e.g. a colour-based segmentation) could be necessary.

Similarly, the method proposed in this manuscript could be used for *RoboCup World Championship and Conference (RoboCup)* [45]. It is an international robotics competition founded in 1997, whose aim is to develop autonomous robots with the intention of promoting research and education in the field of artificial intelligence and intelligent robotics research. For that, it provides a standard problem where a wide range of technologies can be integrated and examined, as well as being used for integrated project-oriented education.

For that purpose, RoboCup decided to use soccer game as a primary domain, where various technologies must be incorporated such as, for instance, design principles of autonomous agents, multi-agent collaboration, strategy acquisition, real-time reasoning, robotics, and sensor fusion. Nevertheless, RoboCup has currently four major domains:

1. RoboCupSoccer, focused on competitive football, has the purpose of developing autonomous soccer robots by means of different technologies:

   - Simulation League ($2D$, $3D$, $3D$ development and mixed reality)
   - Small Size Robot League
   - Middle Size Robot League
   - Four-Legged Robot League
   - Humanoid League (Kid-size and Teen-size)

Fig. 4.7 Foreground-background segmentation in a soccer match video sequence by using the **MoD** approach

Fig. 4.8 Example of images
captured by a camera located
downwards at the top of the
field center

- RoboCup Commentator Exhibition

2. RoboCupRescue, aimed at disaster rescue, intends to build heterogeneous robot
teams that help in search and rescue tasks in a hostile environment. So, multi-
agent team work coordination, physical robotic agent development, and information infrastructures are some of the issues to be solved at different levels. Two
projects and leagues are currently proceeding:

- Rescue Simulation League
- Rescue Robot League

2. RoboCup@Home has as goal developing autonomous service and assistive
robots. So, topics such as Human-Robot interaction (HRI), cooperation, nav-
igation, and mapping in dynamic environments, computer vision, and object
recognition under natural light conditions, object manipulation, adaptive behaviors, behavior integration, or ambient intelligent, are included
3. RoboCupJunior refers to an educational initiative that introduces young people
to the field of Robotics. For that, it provides several challenges:

- Soccer Challenge
- Dance Challenge
- Rescue Challenge

In particular, in some leagues of the RoboCupSoccer domain, a moving object
identification is required in order to know the localization and position of all the
components of the match, that is, the ball and the football players. So, ball tracking
is carried out by means of an external camera, located downwards at the top of the
field center (see Fig. 4.8). The segmentation process usually implies to distinguish an
orange ball on a green background or a pink ball on a gray background, by depending
on the league. However, some conditions such as small changes in illumination can
make it fail. This issue is overcome by the method presented in this manuscript. For

Fig. 4.9 Foreground-background segmentation when a soccer game between teams of 3 small size robots [46] by using the **MoD** approach is analysed

this reason, the algorithm performance has also been evaluated on a video sequence of this nature. Note that, as we have not participated in any of these kinds of competitions, the used video sequence does not provide exactly the described view, although it is useful for the planned experiment.

So, the video sequence of the 3-versus-3 small size robot game between the *Leonding Micros* and *Team Austro* of the Institute for Handling Devices and Robotics (IHRT) from Vienna, celebrated on 4th May in 2007 was used [46]. Some of the obtained results are shown in Fig. 4.9. Note that, as there is no initial frame without foreground elements, the robots are detected when they start moving. That is why they are gradually detected along the different frames. Again, detected foreground elements are enclosed in their minimum bounding rectangle in red.

References

1. Kiryati, N., Raviv, T., Ivanchenko, Y., Rochel, S.: Real-time abnormal motion detection in surveillance video. In: The 19th International Conference on Pattern Recognition (ICPR). Tampa, Florida, USA (2008)
2. Abdelkader, M., Chellappa, R., Zheng, Q., Chan, A.: Integrated motion detection and tracking for visual surveillance. In: Fourth IEEE International Conference on Computer Vision Systems (ICVS), p. 28. New York, USA (2006)
3. Stauffer, C., Grimson, W.: Learning patterns of activity using real-time tracking. IEEE Transactions on Pattern Analysis and Machine Intelligence (PAMI) **27**(5), 747–757 (2000)
4. Wren, C., Azarbeyejani, A., Darrell, T., Pentland, A.: Pfinder: Real-time tracking of the human body. IEEE Transactions on Pattern Analysis and Machine Intelligence (PAMI) **19**(7), 780–785 (1997).
5. Hua, W., Li, P.: Polygon change detection for spot5 color image using multi-feature-clustering-analysis. In: Sixth International Conference on Fuzzy Systems and Knowledge Discovery (FSKD), pp. 260–263. Tianjin, China (2009)
6. Ramachandra, T., Kumar, U.: Geographic resources decision support system for land use, land cover dynamics analysis. In: FOSS/GRASS Users Conference. Bangkok, Thailand (2004)

7. Prenzel, B., Treitz, P.: Remote sensing of land-cover and land-use change for a complex tropical watershed in north sulawesi, indonesia. Remote Sensing for Mapping Land-Cover and Land-Use Change **61**(4), 349–363 (2004)

8. Bruzzone, L., Prieto, D.: An adaptive semiparametric and context-based approach to unsupervised change detection in multitemporal remote-sensing images. IEEE Transactions on Image Processing **11**(4), 452–466 (2002)

9. Seo, H., Milanfar, P.: A non-parametric approach to automatic change detection in mri images of the brain. In: The Sixth IEEE International Symposium on Biomedical Imaging: From Nano to Macro (ISBI). Boston, Massachusets, USA (2009)

10. Rousseau, F., Faisan, S., Heitz, F., Armspach, J., Y. Chevalier, F. Blanc, Seze, J., Rumbach, L.: An a contario approach for change detection in 3d multimodal images: Application to multiple sclerosis in mri. IEEE Engineering in Medicine and Biology Society (EMBS) pp. 2069–2072 (2007)

11. Patriarche, J., Erickson, B.: Part 1. automated change detection and characterization in serial mr studies of brain tumor patients. Journal of Digital Imaging **20**, 203–222 (2007)

12. Landis, E., Zhang, T., Nagy, E., Nagy, G., Franklin, W.: Cracking, damage and fracture in four dimensions. Materials and Structures **40**, 357–364 (2007)

13. Landis, E., Nagy, E., Keane, D.: Microstructure and fracture in three dimensions. Engineering Fracture Mechanics **70**, 911–925 (2003)

14. Nagy, G., Zhang, T., Franklin, W., Landis, E., Nagy, E., Keane, D.: Volume and surface area distributions of cracks in concrete. In: IWVF4, Lecture Notes in Computer Science (LNCS) 2059, pp. 759–768. Springer-Verlag Berlin / Heidelberg (2001)

15. Qi, Z., Cooperstock, J.: Automated change detection in an undersea environment using a statistical background model. In: MTS/IEEE Oceans Conference. Vancouver, BC, Canada (2007)

16. Williams, R., Lambert, T., Kelsall, A., Pauly, T.: Detecting marine animals in underwater video: Let's start with salmon. In: Twelfth Americas Conference on Information Systems, pp. 1482–1490. Acapulco, Mexico (2006)

17. Edgington, D., Salamy, K., Risi, M., Sherlock, R., Walther, D., Christof, K.: Automated event detection in underwater video. In: MTS/IEEE Oceans Conference. San Diego, California (2003)

18. Barris, S., Button, C.: A review of vision-based motion analysis in sport. Sports Medicine **38**, 1025–1043 (19) (2008)

19. Fang, C., Chen, C., Cherng, S., Chen, S.: Critical motion detection of nearby moving vehicles in a vision-based driver assistance system. IEEE Transactions on Intelligent Transportation Systems **10**, 70–82 (2009)

20. Yen, P., Fang, C., Chen, S.: Motion analysis of nearby vehicles on a freeway. In: IEEE International Conference on Networking, Sensing and Control, vol. 2, pp. 903–908 (2004)

21. Fang, C., Chen, S., Fuh, C.: Automatic change detection of driving environments in a vision-based driver assistance system. IEEE Transactions on Neural Networks **14**, 646–657 (2003)

22. Tinbergen, N.: On aims and methods in ethology. Zeitschrift fur Tierpsychologie **20**(4), 410–433 (1963)

23. Partan, S.: http://helios.hampshire.edu/~srpCS/Home.html (2009)

24. Atkociunas, E., Blake, R., Juozapavicius, A., Kazimianec, M.: Image processing in road traffic analysis. Nonlinear Analysis: Modelling and Control **10**(4), 315–332 (2005)

25. Cheung, S., Kamath, C.: Robust techniques for background subtraction in urban traffic video. Electronic Imaging: Video Communications and Image Processing **5308**(1), 881–892 (2004)

26. Kastrinaki, V., Zervakis, M., Kalaitzakis, K.: A survey of video processing techniques for traffic applications. Image and Vision Computing **21**(4), 359–381 (2003)

27. Fathy, M., Siyal, M.: A window-based image processing technique for quantitative and qualitative analysis of road traffic parameters. IEEE Transactions on Vehicular Technology **47**(4), 1342–1349 (1998)

28. Nagel, H.H.: http://i21www.ira.uka.de/image_sequences/

29. Seo, H.J., Milanfar, P.: Detection of human actions from a single example. In: IEEE International Conference on Computer Vision (ICCV), pp. 1965–1970. Kyoto (2009)
30. Moeslund, T., Granum, E.: A survey of computer vision-based human motion capture. Computer Vision and Image Understanding (CVIU) - Modeling people toward vision-based understanding of a person's shape, appearance, and movement **81**, 231–268 (2001)
31. Moeslund, T., Hilton, A., Krüger, V.: A survey of advances in vision-based human motion capture and analysis. Computer Vision and Image Understanding (CVIU) **104**, 90–126 (2006)
32. Poppe, R.: Vision-based human motion analysis: An overview. Computer Vision and Image Understanding **108**, 4–18 (2007)
33. Turaga, P., Chellappa, R., Subrahmanian, V., Udrea, O.: Machine recognition of human activities: A survey. IEEE Transactions on Circuits and Systems for Video Technology **18**, 1473–1488 (2008)
34. Farin, D., Krabbe, S., de With, P., Effelsberg, W.: Robust camera calibration for sport videos using court models. In: SPIE Electronic Imaging, vol. 5307, pp. 80–91. San Jose, CA, USA (2004)
35. Farin, D., Han, J., de With, P.: Fast camera calibration for the analysis of sport sequences. In: IEEE International Conference on Multimedia and Expo (ICME) (2005)
36. Ohta, Y., Kitahara, I., Kameda, Y., Ishikawa, H., Koyama, T.: Live 3d video in soccer stadium. International Journal of Computer Vision **75**, 173–187 (2007)
37. Ali, A., Farrally, M.: A computer-video aided time motion analysis technique for match analysis. Sports Medicine and Physical Fitness **13**, 82–88 (1991).
38. Erdmann, W.: Gathering of kinematic data of sport event by televising the whole pitch and track. In: 10th International Society of Biomechanics in Sports Symposium (ISBS), pp. 159–162. Milan, Italy (1992)
39. Hill, A.: The physiological basis of athletic records. The Scientific Monthly **21**, 409–428 (1925)
40. Keller, J.: Optimal velocity in a race. American Mathematical Monthly **81**, 474–480 (1974)
41. Richards, J.: The measurement of human motion: A comparison of commercially available systems. Human Movement Science **18**, 589–602 (1999)
42. Pers, J., Vuckovic, G., Kovacic, S., Dezman, B.: A low-cost real-time tracker of live sport events. In: International Symposium of Image and Signal Processing and, Analysis, pp. 362–365 (2001)
43. Vuèkoviè, G., Dezman, B., Erculj, F., Kovacic, S., Pers, J.: Differences between the winning and the losing players in a squash game in terms of distance covered. In: The Eighth International Table Tennis Federation Sports Science Congress and The Third World Congress of Science and Racket Sports, pp. 202–207 (2004)
44. Bon, M., Šibila, M., Pori, P.: Sagit computer vision system for tracking handball players during the match. In: EURO 2004 Coaches' Seminar during the 2004 Men's European Championship. Slovenia (2004)
45. Robocup world championship and conference. http://www.robocup.org/ (1997)
46. TeamLeondingMicros: A 3 versus 3 mirosot game between the leonding micros and team austro of the ihrt institute from vienna. http://www.youtube.com/watch?v=QhmehYb2Rtg (2007)

Chapter 5
Appendix: Computer Vision Concepts

Abstract In this chapter, we will introduce some of the concepts and techniques of Computer Vision that are used throughout this book. This description does not represent an exhaustive introduction into the Computer Vision field, but it is addressed to clarify those terms to a reader unfamiliar with them.

Keywords Machine vision · Computer vision · Image segmentation · Background subtraction · Motion detection · Robot vision · Dynamic environments · Visual surveillance · Computer vision terms · Color spaces · Thresholding methods

5.1 Color Spaces

Humans use color information to distinguish objects, materials, food, places, and even the time of day. So, color provides multiple measurements at a single pixel of the image, often enabling classification to be done without complex spatial decision making.

It has been long recognized that, as perceived by most human observers, any color of light can be specified by stating three numerical values. That is, color is *three-dimensional* in the mathematical (not geometric) sense. There are, however, many different schemes of coordinates under which these three numerical values might be defined. These schemes, when fully specified as to their details, are called *color spaces*.

5.1.1 RGB Space

The *trichromatic* Red-Green-Blue (RGB) encoding in graphics system is generally used to represent colors in devices which emit light, such as screen displays. Actually, the RGB color space is an additive color model in which red, green, and blue light are

E. Martínez-Martín and A. P. del Pobil, *Robust Motion Detection in Real-Life Scenarios*, 99
SpringerBriefs in Computer Science, DOI: 10.1007/978-1-4471-4216-4_5,
© Ester Martínez-Martín 2012

Fig. 5.1 A representation
of additive color mixing.
Overlap of primary colors
shows secondary colors;
while the combination of all
three (*red*, *green* and *blue*) in
appropriate intensities makes
white

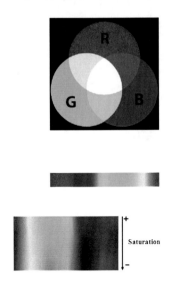

Fig. 5.2 A range of hues such
that *red*, *blue* or *yellow* color
can be easily identified

Fig. 5.3 Sample of saturation
effect on different colors by
showing high saturation colors
at the *top* and low saturation
colors at the *bottom*

added together in various ways to reproduce a broad array of colours (see Fig. 5.1). Nevertheless, it is a *device-dependent* color space such that different devices detect or reproduce a given RGB value differently because the color elements (such as phosphors or dyes) and their response to the individual R, G, and B levels vary from manufacturer to manufacturer, or even in the same device over time. Thus, an RGB value does not define the same color across devices without some kind of color management and this makes it not appropriate for image processing.

5.1.2 HSI Color Space

The Hue-Saturation-Intensity (HSI) system, sometimes referred to as the *HSV* system, encodes color information by separating out an overall intensity value I from two values encoding *chromaticity*—hue H and saturation S- such that:

- **Hue (H)** is the name of a distinct color of the spectrum, that is, it is the particular wavelength frequency that identifies the color red, green, yellow, orange, blue, and so on. A range of hues is depicted in Fig. 5.2 where it is easy to point to *red*, *blue*, or *yellow*.
- **Saturation (S)** defines the amount of white to be mixed with the color. For example, dark chocolate is a brown (hue) with little saturation, whereas milk chocolate is brown (hue) with greater saturation. So, as saturation decreases, all colours become a value of gray (see Fig. 5.3).
- **Intensity (I)** is the amount of light or white a color contains. Thus, when light is at its fullest intensity, colors will become bright, while, at its least intensity, colors

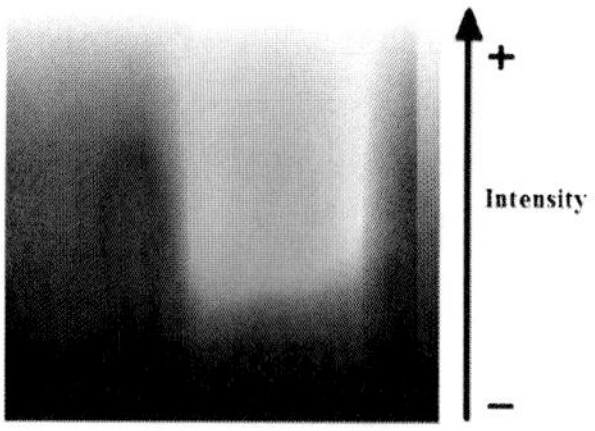

Fig. 5.4 Sample of intensity influence on different colors so a higher value creates a whiter, brighter color

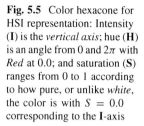

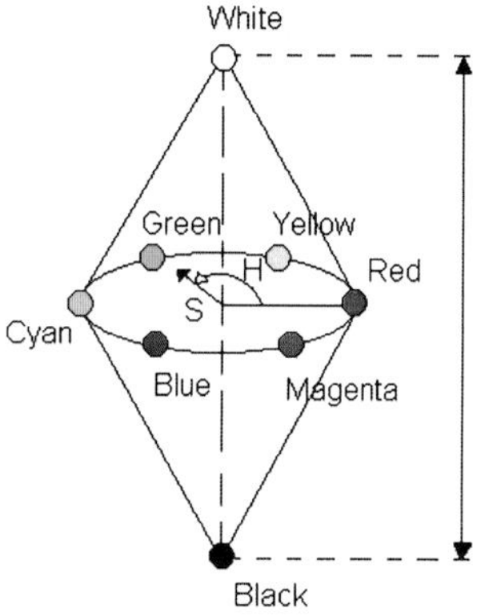

Fig. 5.5 Color hexacone for HSI representation: Intensity (**I**) is the *vertical axis*; hue (**H**) is an angle from 0 and 2π with *Red* at 0.0; and saturation (**S**) ranges from 0 to 1 according to how pure, or unlike *white*, the color is with $S = 0.0$ corresponding to the **I**-axis

become dim. Unlike saturation, there is not necessarily *less* of the color—it is just not as intense, as it is shown in Fig. 5.4.

A 3D representation, depicted in Fig. 5.5, allows us to visualize the former cube diagonal as a vertical intensity axis *I*. *H* is defined by an angle between 0 and 2π relative to the red-axis, with pure red at an angle of 0, pure green at $2\pi/3$ and pure blue at $4\pi/3$. *S* is the *third* coordinate value needed in order to completely specify a point in this color space.

Note that HSI is more convenient to graphic design because it provides direct control of brightness and hue. Moreover, it might also provide better support for computer vision algorithms because it can normalize for lighting and focus on the two chromaticity parameters that are more associated with the intrinsic character of a surface rather than the source that is lighting it.

Derivation of *HSI* coordinates from *RGB* ones is given by the Algorithm 1. Note that *S* is not defined when $I = 0$ and *H* is not defined when $S = 0$.

5.1.3 CIE Lab Space

CIE Lab space is the most complete color space specified by the International Commission on Illumination (*Commission Internationale d'Eclairage*, hence its CIE initialism). It describes all the colors visible to the human eye and was created to

Algorithm 1 Conversion of RGB encoding to HSI encoding

$I = max\,(R, G, B)$;
$min = min\,(R, G, B)$;
if $(I \geq 0.0)$ **then**
  $S = \frac{(I-min)}{S}$;
else
  $S = 0.0$;
end if
if $(S \leq 0.0)$ **then**
  $H = -1.0$;
  return;
end if
$diff = I - min$;
if $(R == I)$ **then**
  $H = \frac{(\pi/3)+\pi/3*(G-B)}{diff}$;
else if $(G == I)$ **then**
  $H = \frac{(2*\pi/3)+\pi/3*(B-R)}{diff}$;
else if $(B == I)$ **then**
  $H = \frac{(4*\pi/3)+\pi/3*(R-G)}{diff}$;
end if
if $(H \leq 0.0)$ **then**
  $H = H + 2\pi$;
end if

serve as a device-independent model to be used as a reference. Strongly influenced by the Munsell color system, the intention of *Lab* color space is creating a space which can be computed via simple formulas from the *XYZ space*, but is more perceptually uniform than *XYZ*. In this context, perceptually uniform means that a change of the same amount in a color value will produce a change of about the same visual importance.

Lab color space is described by three coordinates: the lightness of the color ($L = 0$ yields black and $L = 100$ indicates diffuse white; specular white may be higher), its position between red/magenta and green (*a*, negative values indicate green while positive values indicate magenta) and its position between yellow and blue (*b*, negative values indicate blue and positive values indicate yellow). That is, it is a color-opponent space with dimension L for lightness and *a* and *b* for the colour-opponent dimensions, based on nonlinearly compressed *CIE XYZ color space coordinates*. CIE Lab is a chromatic value color space since its opponent channels are computed as differences of lightness transformations of (putative) cone responses.

The tristimulus values of this color space are obtained from the XYZ coordinates as follows:

$$\begin{cases} L = 116f\left(\frac{Y}{Y_n}\right) - 16 \\ a = 500\left[f\left(\frac{X}{X_n}\right) - f\left(\frac{Y}{Y_n}\right)\right] \\ b = 200\left[f\left(\frac{Y}{Y_n}\right) - f\left(\frac{Z}{Z_n}\right)\right] \end{cases} \tag{5.1}$$

where

$$f(t) = \begin{cases} t^{\frac{1}{3}} & \text{if } t > (\frac{6}{29})^3 \\ \frac{1}{3}(\frac{6}{29})^2 t + \frac{4}{29} & \text{otherwise} \end{cases} \tag{5.2}$$

such that X_n, Y_n, and Z_n are the CIE XYZ tristimulus values of the reference white point (the subscript n suggests *normalized*).

5.2 Thresholding Methods

5.2.1 Basic Thresholding

It is done by visiting each pixel site in the image, and set the pixel to maximum value if its value is above or equal to a given threshold and to minimum value if the threshold value is below the pixel values:

$$I_t(x) = \begin{cases} 1 & \text{if } T \leq I(x) \\ 0 & \text{otherwise} \end{cases} \quad \text{or} \quad I_t(x) = \begin{cases} 1 & \text{if } T \geq I(x) \\ 0 & \text{otherwise} \end{cases} \tag{5.3}$$

5.2.2 Band Thresholding

This method is similar to *basic thresholding*, but has two threshold values, and set the pixel site to maximum value if pixel intensity value is between or at the threshold values, else it is set to minimum:

$$I_t(x) = \begin{cases} 1 & \text{if } T_a \leq I(x) \leq T_b \\ 0 & \text{otherwise} \end{cases} \tag{5.4}$$

5.3 Connected Component Labeling

Although there are several connected component labeling algorithms, a *row-by-row* labeling method [1] is used to reduce the computational cost of the whole process. A very simple example of this process is depicted in Fig. 5.6. Thus, the binary image, by resulting from the segmentation process, is scanned twice:

• The first time to temporally tag each foreground pixel and store equivalences between labels. When a new foreground pixel is visited, tag to be assigned is calculated by basing on the labels of its visited neighbors as follows:

   – neither of its neighbors is tagged: a new label is generated
   – all of its tagged neighbors have the same label: the same tag is assigned to the current pixel

(a)

1	1	0	1	1	1	0	1
1	1	0	1	0	1	0	1
1	1	1	1	0	0	0	1
0	0	0	0	0	0	0	1
1	1	1	1	0	1	0	1
0	0	0	1	0	1	0	1
1	1	0	1	0	0	0	1
1	1	0	1	0	1	1	1

(b)

1	1	0	2	2	2	0	3
1	1	0	2	0	2	0	3
1	1	1	1	0	0	0	3
0	0	0	0	0	0	0	3
4	4	4	4	0	5	0	3
0	0	0	4	0	5	0	3
6	6	0	4	0	0	0	3
6	6	0	4	0	7	7	3

(c)

1	1	0	1	1	1	0	3
1	1	0	1	0	1	0	3
1	1	1	1	0	0	0	3
0	0	0	0	0	0	0	3
4	4	4	4	0	5	0	3
0	0	0	4	0	5	0	3
6	6	0	4	0	0	0	3
6	6	0	4	0	3	3	3

Fig. 5.6 Simple example of row-by-row algorithm

- its neighbor labels are different: the current pixel is tagged with one of them and a correspondence between them is stored

- The second crossed scan is to unify tags which belongs to the same blob. It is possible thanks to the correspondence table stored in the previous scan.

5.4 Convolution

The convolution of two functions $f(x, y)$ and $h(x, y)$ is defined as follows:

$$g(x, y) = f(x, y) * h(x, y) \equiv \int\limits_{x'=-\infty}^{+\infty} \int\limits_{y'=-\infty}^{+\infty} f(x', y') h(x - x', y - y') dx'dy'$$

(5.5)

such that convolution is defined formally in terms of continuous picture functions. In order for the integrals to be defined and to have practical use, the $2D$ image functions $f(x, y)$ and $h(x, y)$ should have zero values outside of some finite rectangle in the xy-plane and have finite volume under their surface. For filtering, the *kernel* function $h(x, y)$ will often be zero outside some rectangle that is much smaller than the rectangle that supports $f(x, y)$. In particular, when images are considered, convolution changes the intensities of a pixel to reflect the intensities of the surrounding pixels. In this case, discrete sums of products instead of the continuous integrals are used (see Fig. 5.7).

5.5 Morphological Operations

The operations of binary morphology input a binary image **B** and a *structuring element* **S**, and result in another binary image. The structuring element represents a shape, such as, for instance, the ones shown in the Fig. 5.8; it can be of any size

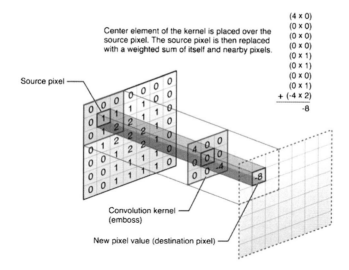

Fig. 5.7 Kernel convolution example on an image (courtesy of Apple-Inc. [2])

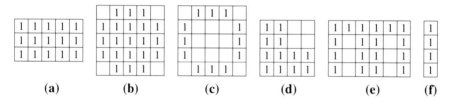

Fig. 5.8 Examples of structuring elements (*blanks* represent 0s)

and have arbitrary structure that can be represented by a binary image. However, there are a number of common structuring elements such as a rectangle of specified dimensions or a circular region of specified diameter. The purpose of the structuring elements is to act as probes of the binary image. One pixel of the structuring element is denoted as its *origin*; this is often the central pixel of a symmetric structuring element, but can in principle be any chosen pixel. Using the origin as a reference point, translation of the structuring element can be placed anywhere on the image and can be used to either enlarge a region by that shape or to check whether or not the shape fits inside a region. For instance, we might want to check the size of holes by seeing if a smaller disk fits entirely within a region, while a larger disk does not.

5.5.1 Basic Operations

The basic operations of binary morphology are:

- *Dilation*. It enlarges a region by turning foreground pixels that were originally background. Mathematically, the dilation of a binary image **B** by a structuring element **S** is denoted by $B \oplus S$ and is defined by:

$$B \oplus S = \bigcup_{b \in B} S_b \qquad (5.6)$$

  This union can be thought as a neighborhood operator. The structuring element **S** is swept over the image. Each time the origin of the structuring element touches a binary 1-pixel, the entire translated structuring element shape is written in the output image, which has been initialized to all zeros. Figure 5.9a shows a binary image, and Fig. 5.9c illustrates its dilation by the 3×3 rectangular structuring element depicted in Fig. 5.9b

- *Erosion*. It removes pixels from an image or, equivalently, turns background pixels that were originally foreground. The purpose is to remove pixels that should not be there. The simplest example is pixels that have been selected by thresholding because they fall into the brightness range of interest, but do not lie within the regions of that brightness. Instead, they can have that brightness value either accidentally, because of finite noise in the image, or because they happen to straddle a boundary between a lighter and darker region and thus have an averaged brightness that happens to lie on the range selected by thresholding. Formally, the erosion of a binary image **B** by a structuring element **S** is denoted by $B \ominus S$ and is defined by:

$$B \ominus S = \{b | b + s \in B \forall s \in S\} \qquad (5.7)$$

  The erosion operation also sweeps the structuring element over the entire image. At each position where every 1-pixel of the structuring element covers a 1-pixel of the binary image, the binary image pixel corresponding to the origin of the structuring element is kept in the output image. Figure 5.9d illustrates an erosion of the binary image of Fig. 5.9a by the 3×3 rectangular structuring element (Fig. 5.9b)

- *Closing*. It is the result of combining a dilation followed by an erosion. Basically, it closes up narrow gaps between portions of a feature or missing pixels within features, by filling in places where isolated pixels were classified as background. In a more formal way, the closing of a binary image **B** by a structuring element **S** is denoted by $B \bullet S$ and is defined by:

$$B \bullet S = (B \oplus S) \ominus S \qquad (5.8)$$

An example of the result of the closing operation of a binary image (Fig. 5.9a) by a 3×3 rectangular structuring element (Fig. 5.9b) is depicted in Fig. 5.9e.

Fig. 5.9 The basic operations of binary morphology (dilation, erosion, closing, and opening) of a binary image **B** by a structuring element **S**. Foreground pixels are labeled with 1 s; while background pixels, whose value is 0, are shown as *blanks*

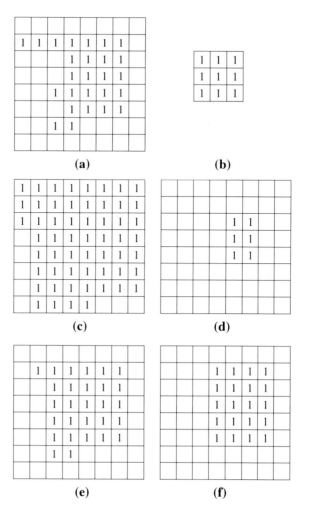

(a)   (b)

(c)   (d)

(e)   (f)

- *Opening*. It is the combination of an erosion followed by a dilation. The ability of this combination is to open up spaces between just-touching features. For that reason, it is one of the most commonly used sequences for removing noisy pixels from binary images. Note that parameters of erosion and dilation operations are kept the same. From a mathematical point of view, the opening of a binary image **B** by a structuring element **S** is denoted as $B \circ S$ and is expressed as:

$$B \circ S = (B \ominus S) \oplus S \qquad (5.9)$$

Figure 5.9f illustrates the opening of a binary image (Fig. 5.9a) by the 3×3 rectangular structuring element shown in Fig. 5.9b.

References

1. Shapiro, L., Stockman, G.: Computer vision. Prentice Hall (2001)
2. Apple-Inc.: http://developer.apple.com/library/mac/navigation/ (2010)

Printed by Publishers' Graphics LLC
MO20120821